Lost League Football Grounds
2nd edition
Martin Plumb and Ken Coton

© Martin Plumb & Ken Coton 2017

ISBN 978 071103 8660

First published 2017 by Crécy Publishing Ltd

A CIP record for this book is available from the British Library.

Publisher's Note: Every effort has been made to identify and correctly attribute photographic credits. Any error that may have occurred is entirely unintentional.

Printed in Poland by Opolgraf

Crécy Publishing Limited
1a Ringway Trading Estate
Shadowmoss Road
Manchester M22 5LH

www.crecy.co.uk

Below left: Bradford Park Avenue in 1987. (P.22)

Title page: Leicester City, Filbert Street, Main Stand, 1976. (P.74)

Front Cover:
West Ham's Boleyn Ground
1 - ARSENAL, Highbury - East Stand - 1965
2 - HULL, Boothferry Park - East Stand / Kempton Stand - 1986
3 - CRAWLEY, Town Mead -1950s
4 - DAGENHAM, Victoria Road - North Stand - 1993
5 - MIDDLESBROUGH, Ayresome Park - West Stand - 1987
6 - SOUTHAMPTON, The Dell - Archers Road End - 1967

Back cover:
Walsall's Fellows Park
1 - WORKINGTON, Borough Park - Main Stand - 1987
2 - SUNDERLAND, Roker Park - Clock Side and Fulwell End - 1979
3 - COVENTRY, Highfield Road - Thackhall Street Stand - 1996
4 - MANCHESTER, Maine Road - Platt Lane End - 1970s
5 - LINCOLN, Sincil Bank - Main Stand / St Andrews Stand - 1993

Contents

West Ham, the old West Stand, 1960s.

Introduction to the Second Edition

This book builds on the trilogy that started in 1994 with *Football Grounds Then and Now* (Dial House, out of print) and continued a decade later with *Football Grounds Fact Book* (Ian Allan Publishing, also out of print). As its title suggests, this volume and the previous edition (*Lost League Football Grounds*, Ian Allan Publishing, 2010) concentrate on grounds which once hosted league football but do so no longer, because either the club that played there no longer exists, or has lost its league status or – an increasingly common occurrence these days – has moved to a more modern ground with improved facilities and access, coupled with the demands of new regulations. Some of these clubs could of course return to Football League status where circumstances permit and when achievements are fulfilled. This edition also includes

Bolton Wanderers' Burnden Park, Darcy Lever Stand, September 1969. (P.18)

grounds of teams who currently have Football League status, but whose ground was lost whilst they were a non-league side.

This book provides new static and action shots for the vast majority of grounds featured in the first edition. With the cyclical nature of our national sport, some grounds have disappeared from that edition, whilst several new entries have arrived.

The book's primary aim is to provide a snapshot of the teams that comprise the English Football League at the beginning of the 2016–17 season. The secondary aim is to also include clubs that have left the Football League. Scottish sides and grounds have been omitted from this edition, because of the significant number of new entries from the English Football League.

Most clubs led a nomadic existence during the period 1880–1910, and often occupied several temporary sites. There are passing references to these sites, but the book focuses on a club's main, settled and permanent location.

Whilst the book concentrates on stadia, the clubs that occupy them and their fluctuating fortunes are inextricably intertwined. The changes relating to a club's status very often influence and affect the infrastructure of its home ground. As far as possible, such significant events and times are included. Throughout the book, strenuous effort has been made to correctly name stands featured in the pictures, but with some images this has proved difficult, particularly for stands that have been demolished, rebuilt or renovated. Apologies are extended to fans offended by any mis-identification; this will be happily corrected in the next edition.

Where grounds themselves have been renamed due to sponsorship, the current name is included.

Changes of the names of individual stands due to sponsorship occur regularly these days, but such changes are outside the scope of this book. The 'mostly known' name is included. Similarly, the use of stands for home, away, family and disabled spectators changes just as rapidly, so only limited references are included.

With the ever-changing names of the various leagues within the football pyramid over the last 25 years due to sponsorship or re-organisation, the book assumes some basic knowledge of the football hierarchy throughout the period.

The comfort and safety of spectators shot to the top of the table, so to speak, after the twin horrors of Bradford (1985) and Hillsborough (1989), when all-seater stadia became mandatory for the higher divisions. The huge costs associated with bringing old, rusting and cramped stadia into line with the new Taylor Report regulations meant that remaining in situ was for many clubs simply a non-starter, a new stadium sometimes being less expensive than a 'make do and mend' option at their original home.

The financial imperatives of the modern game also dictate that clubs must increase their matchday revenue, and that means getting more fans through the gate into bigger, purpose-built arenas. It was this that motivated Arsenal and may yet one day persuade the likes of Everton to leave their traditional and much-loved homes in favour of larger stadia. There is also a growing necessity for new stadiums to be increasingly community-based, with facilities that can be utilised on non-matchdays.

While many old grounds are now supermarkets or housing estates, it is important to remember that, in the past, these sites once played host to significant and memorable moments in British football history,

where leagues were won and lost, scenes of promotion and relegation were witnessed, and joy and despair were experienced in equal measure. They were places that generations called home on a Saturday afternoon, where families came together to support the club they loved so dearly.

While some of these redeveloped sites pay homage to their former status as sporting battlegrounds with a sole remaining floodlight or a plaque where the centre circle once stood, others bear absolutely no trace of the history that went before. In a world of concrete identikit and sometimes out-of-town stadiums, traditional football grounds intrinsically linked to the local population are fast becoming few and far between.

While the relentless march of progress cannot be halted, and new grounds are undeniably better equipped, many fans believe a little of their club's heart and soul fails to survive such transitions. And it's certainly a source of regret to fans of a certain age that the locations where they witnessed football history in the making are now superstores, or flats and houses. We hope that this book's words and pictures will bring back memories for 'oldies' while educating younger fans as to where their club has, literally, come from to be where it is today.

So join us on a journey of nostalgia through endless Main Stands, Spion Kops, Popular Sides and Cowsheds, many originally built on council rubbish tips or farmland potato fields that survived wartime bombings. The journey encompasses fires and floods, frauds and financial crises, as we take a look at these unique pieces of history that represent what is, to many, football's golden era.

Above left: Holker Street, Barrow, Main Stand 1964. (P.16)

Left: Plough Lane, Wimbledon, South Stand, 1989. (P.138)

Both main stands at Somerton Park, Newport, 1995. (P.94)

Acknowledgements

Sincere thanks are given to the following people and organisations who have contributed to this book.

On the pictorial side:

Mark Sheldrake for his assistance and the use of his extensive personal archive;
Ian Thomson of *www.legendaryfootballgrounds.com* for the use of that website's images;

Ken Coton for providing action pictures from his archive – *www.ashwaterpress.co.uk*;
Wikimedia Commons images as follows:
Christopher Elkins – Twerton Park (page 155);
Jem – Withdean Stadium (page 154);
Nick MacNeill – National Hockey Stadium (page 159);
Matthew Hatton – Don Valley Stadium (page 158);
Steve Daniels – Yeovil 1983 (page 149);
Crawley Town pictures courtesy of *www.ctfchistory.co.uk.*

The copyright of all images is acknowledged.

On the text side:

Joanna Plumb for her research assistance and proof-reading.
Dave Wilson for his input, expertise and proof-reading.

Martin Plumb and Ken Coton 2017

Moss Rose Macclesfield, Star Lane End, 1993, before the covered stand. (P.80)

Highest attendance: 17,634 v Blackburn Rovers (Friendly), 15 November 1954

First league match: Accrington Stanley 4-0 v Rochdale, 3 September 1921

Final league match: Accrington Stanley 0-2 v Rochdale, 24 February 1962 (result expunged)

Ground layout: Burnley Road Side, Hotel Side, Kop End, Huncoat End

Status: Demolished

Current stadium: Crown Ground (Wham Stadium)

Peel Park, ideally situated at a convenient spot in the town, was home to the first incarnation of Accrington Stanley from 1919 to 1966, when the club resigned from the Football League mid-season. A similar fate had befallen rivals and founding league members Accrington FC in 1893, the club resigning from the League after relegation from the top flight.

The Peel family, one of whom was Sir Robert Peel (credited as being the founder of the British Police Force), were successful business people in the world of calico printing. They owned the Accrington land on which Stanley Street was built and also the surrounding land. The ground was therefore named after the family. The club were able to buy the site for £2,500 in 1919.

Accrington Stanley were so called because their first meetings were held in the Stanley Arms pub in Stanley Street. Many of the Stanley Villa team came from the Working Men's Club in Stanley Street who then took the town's name to become Accrington Stanley. Established in 1891, the club played in the Football League between 1921 and 1962.

The pitch at Peel Park was narrow and cramped and possessed a notorious slope.

The club were the first to experiment with floodlights in 1954, perched on eight telegraph poles at a cost of £4,000, ahead of their illustrious neighbours Blackburn and Burnley. Stanley's attempt at the first-ever floodlit game in British football drew a record crowd of 17,634 for a friendly against Blackburn Rovers, and these were the glory days for Peel Park. The highest league attendance, 15,428, came the following April in 1955 versus York City. Also in 1955 a Third Division North versus South match was televised from Peel Park by the BBC with Kenneth Wolstenholme commentating.

Ambitious plans for a new two-tier stand at the Burnley Road side, including a suite of offices and a ballroom, were drawn up, and then shelved. Instead, Stanley purchased the second-hand 4,000-seat main stand from the Aldershot Military Tattoo in 1958. The dismantling, transportation and re-erection of the stand – in which viewing was virtually impossible from some angles – brought the total cost to nearly £20,000, more expensive than if the club had built a stand itself. It was this new stand for Peel Park that effectively sealed the club's financial demise, being a step too far for a team that never progressed beyond the Third Division.

It was just four years before the club would resign from the Football League mid-season in 1962, with a historical quirk bringing Rochdale to Peel Park for Stanley's final home league game just over four decades since they arrived for their first. Following their expulsion from the League, Accrington Stanley struggled on for four more years in the Lancashire

View of the pitch in the late 1980s/early 1990s.

Combination, before folding in 1966. Peel Park was left abandoned and dilapidated but intact upon Stanley's demise, but in 1972 the Hotel Stand, the oldest structure on the ground built in 1921, was badly damaged by fire and collapsed; it was completely demolished soon afterwards. The Peel Park Kop, a large open concrete terrace dating from the early 1950s, was demolished in the mid-1970s.

The pitch and surrounds still remain to this day and the pitch is now used by the adjacent Peel Park Primary School as a playing field. Appropriately, junior league matches played by Peel Park FC are still using the pitch for football. Surrounding the pitch, the usual daisies and docks battle it out with the sweep of damp grassland. Standing sentinel in the corner is a towering array of silver birch; on the top side there's a bank of hawthorn. Now there's just a ghostly whisper through the trees as a gentle breeze curls down from the Coppice which overlooks the town. In the corner is an old red-brick shed/block, the sort of outbuilding that comes in handy for a school sports ground; it was possibly the changing rooms and contains a stone plaque recording that it was built by the supporters' club in 1937.

In March 2011 a *Time Team* type exercise led to the digging of two trenches at Peel Park, one over part of the original Hotel Side stand and another over the front edge of the Peel Park Kop at the Huncoat End. This led to the recovery of many social artefacts and football ground items from times gone by.

The re-formed Accrington Stanley, founded in 1968, moved to the Crown Ground built that year. Problems with the pitch at the Crown Ground almost led to a return to Peel Park in the early 1970s, but it wasn't to be. Stanley eventually achieved promotion back to the Football League in 2006 and the Crown Ground has since expanded to a 5,000 capacity. The club currently compete in League Two.

Right: Aerial view 1961. Aerofilms

9

Aldershot

Recreation Ground

Address: High Street, Aldershot, Hants
GU11 1TW

Highest attendance: 19,138 v Carlisle
United (FA Cup), 28 January 1970

First league match: Aldershot 1-2
v Southend United, (Aldershot), 27 August
1932

Aldershot 1-1 v Bournemouth,
(Aldershot Town), 16 August 2008

Final league match: Aldershot 0-3 v Lincoln
City, (Aldershot), 14 March 1992
(result expunged)

Aldershot 1-0 v Dagenham & Redbridge
(Aldershot Town), 20 April 2013

International matches: England U-17s

Other usages: Chelsea Reserves,
Reading Reserves, Army FC

Ground layout: North (Main) Stand,
East Bank, South Stand, High Street End

Status: Extant

Current stadium: Recreation Ground
(The EBB Stadium)

Aldershot was a mere village before the Army established a permanent military camp in the area in 1854. Football began as a pastime for soldiers. A football club for officers was in existence in 1863, the year of the formation of the Football Association, but it would take more than 60 years to establish a senior civilian club in the town. Aldershot FC was formed in December 1926, and an application to join the Southern League (Eastern Section) was accepted.

A suitable home venue, albeit a public park and just a pitch with only stone terracing and no stands, was found at the council-owned Recreation Ground in the High Street, close to local facilities and running alongside the main railway line. The amenity was leased from the council. In 1928–29 work was started on the South Stand, still in use today, and the 1929–30 season began with the opening of that stand. After five years the club joined the Football League Third Division South in 1932. The interior of the ground hasn't changed a great deal since the early days of Aldershot FC. The ground itself is situated in a pleasant setting with plenty of trees visible around its perimeter.

The North Stand is the main stand of the Recreation Ground running along one side of the pitch and was built in the late 1930s; it was once all terrace. It houses the players' changing rooms and the club's directors' box and media centre. Adjoining the North Stand are the club offices. There is also a conference room and bar adjacent to the offices behind the North Stand which was constructed in the early 2000s. The stand itself features a combination of terracing and seating. To the east of the stand is a terraced area and to

The North Stand in the 1960s.

the west of the stand is a further terraced area with a disabled bay. In the centre is a large seated area.

The East Bank is the largest stand of the Recreation Ground, capable of holding several thousand fans and has a number of supporting pillars running across the front of it. The design is unusual as it is not like most stands that have a flat roof; instead the roof is barrel-shaped towards the rear, with a flat roof covering the lower parts of the East Bank. This is so because the stand originally had just the barrel-shaped roof and it wasn't until later that a front section was added to cover its lower half.

The South Stand is the only all-seated stand, running for half the length of the pitch and accommodating both home and away fans. This covered stand is the oldest at the ground. It has remained fairly untouched over the past 70 years, although an increase in ground safety regulations has meant that some minor work has been carried out in order for the stand to remain in use. Either side of the stand are open terraces; one, the south west terrace (known amongst fans as 'The Slab') is used by home fans, the other is used by away fans.

Until 2013, the High Street End was unused for spectators, having just a narrow path and some advertising hoardings. However, to help the club comply with League rules stipulating the number of seats that a ground must have, a small prefabricated covered area was erected on one side of this end (towards the Main Stand). Called The Community Stand, it comprises just four rows of seats and only runs from the corner flag to the goal area. It has a total seating capacity of 250. On the other side of this end is a two-storey green Portakabin that serves as a police control box.

The ground benefits from a set of traditional corner floodlight pylons.

At the start of the 1990s, Aldershot Football Club was sinking deeper into financial turmoil after mis-management from a succession of directors. With significant debts, and despite notable gestures for ground sharing from Cardiff City and Swindon Town, the club was formally wound up in the High Court on 25 March 1992. It ceased all fixtures in mid-season, and was obliged to resign from the Football League,

the first club to do so since Accrington Stanley in 1962. The badge disappeared with the sad demise of the club.

From the ashes of the disaster arose Aldershot Town Football Club in the same year. Formed by a committee of fans and local businessmen, the club has relied almost entirely on the patronage of several thousand passionate and loyal fans, sponsorship and advertising. Quite apt then that the current crest of the club is a Phoenix rising from the flames.

The club rose steadily over 15 years and finally re-joined the Football League in 2008, but dropped out once again in 2013, this time due to relegation. The Shots currently compete in the Vanarama National League and succeeded in making the play-offs in 2016–17. For sponsorship reasons the ground became the ESS Stadium (the Electrical Services Stadium); and in August 2015 the ground was renamed the EBB Stadium in a further corporate sponsorship arrangement with the local independent paper supplier. The ground remains in a public park with virtually unrestricted access during the week.

The North Stand in the 1990s.

The South Stand, 1970s.

Arsenal

Highbury

Address: Avenell Road, Highbury, London N5 1BU

Highest attendance: 73,295 v Sunderland, 9 March 1935

First league match: Arsenal 2–1 v Leicester Fosse, 6 September 1913

Final league match: Arsenal 4–2 v Wigan Athletic, 7 May 2006

International matches: England (1921–61)

Other usages: Olympic Games – football (1948), FA Cup semi-finals, Boxing (1966), Rugby League, Baseball (1916–19), Cricket

Ground layout: North Bank, Clock End (South Stand), East Stand, West Stand

Status: Partially demolished

Current stadium: Ashburton Grove (The Emirates Stadium)

Right: The East Stand, October 1965.

Built just before the First World War when Arsenal moved north of the river from Woolwich, and vacated in 2006, Highbury is one of the Premier League stadiums to be replaced by a bigger and better model. From 1919 onwards it hosted only top-flight football. The first incarnation was designed by famed architect Archibald Leitch, well known for his association with British football stadiums, and was funded by the Arsenal chairman Sir Henry Norris.

Highbury (officially titled the Arsenal Stadium) was hurriedly built on the site of a local college's recreation ground and opened towards the end of 1913 with a match against Leicester Fosse. Despite the ground being unfinished, it still attracted attention amongst the football elite. It featured a single stand on the eastern side that housed 9,000 spectators making it at the time the largest stand in London, with the other three sides having banked terracing. However, just seven years later it was regularly hosting England internationals, as well as becoming an FA Cup semi-final venue.

The club bought out the lease to the ground in 1925 for £64,000 and this allowed Highbury to be expanded and tailored to the Gunners' needs. The North Bank terrace was enlarged before the art deco West Stand was completed in 1932 for £45,000 featuring a state-of-the-art two-tiered design that housed 21,000 spectators seated

and standing, resulting in Leitch's original stand being demolished.

Four years later, the East Stand was erected at a massive cost for the time of £130,000. The focal point of Highbury with its imposing façade and famed marble halls, it could seat 8,000 fans and was more than three times as expensive as the West Stand built four years previously. It also housed the directors' area, players' changing rooms and club offices. It also contained three tiers, with the two seated areas raised above a lower terraced paddock.

The famous Highbury clock was originally installed in 1936 at the back of the North Bank (originally called the Gillespie Road End) until it was covered during this same period. The clock was the first of its kind ever to be seen at a football ground. It was relocated to the South Stand (previously known as the College End), thenceforth known as the Clock End. The switch was timely as the North Stand's new roof lasted less than a decade, destroyed by bombing during the Second World War. The roof was not restored until 1956.

Highbury was largely left alone until the 1990s. Floodlights were fitted on the roof of both East and West Stands in 1951, with the first floodlit match being a friendly against Hapoel Tel Aviv on 19 September of that year. In 1964 Arsenal became the first ground to have undersoil heating installed. In 1969 the West Stand was made all seater when 5,500 seats were installed onto the paddock terrace.

In 1989 executive boxes and a roof were added to the Clock End and post-Taylor Report adaptations saw a totally rebuilt North Bank open in 1993 in the art deco style of its older neighbours, seating 12,000 fans in two tiers and featuring a cantilevered roof.

With Highbury now an all-seater stadium, the capacity was capped at slightly over 38,000, around half that of rivals Manchester United. Further attempts at expansion were blocked by the local community. The call for more revenue through gate receipts and corporate opportunity saw Arsenal depart Highbury.

After a failed attempt to purchase Wembley Stadium to share with the England team, the club vacated Highbury for the 60,000-capacity Emirates Stadium in 2006 just a quarter of a mile away from the original home; official reports put the cost of the project at over £470m.

Highbury stadium has since been converted into 711 apartments at a development named Highbury Square, with only the exteriors of the listed East and West Stands remaining, being incorporated into the development. The pitch area remains and has become a communal garden. Arsenal's famous clock was moved from Highbury to the outer side of the new stadium, with a new larger version of the feature added inside the ground in August 2010. Approaching a century in the top flight, Arsenal remain a Premier League force and annual European contenders.

The Clock End, 1988.

The North Bank, 1992.

Address: Westcombe Drive, Barnet, Herts EN5 2DN

Highest attendance: 11,026 v Wycombe Wanderers, 23 February 1952

First league match: Barnet 4-7 v Crewe Alexandra, 17 August 1991

Final league match: Barnet 1-0 v Wycombe Wanderers, 20 April 2013

Other usages: Arsenal Reserves, Edgware Town, Rugby – London Broncos (training)

Ground layout: South Stand, Main Stand, Family Stand, Northwest Terrace, East Stand, North Stand, Northeast Family Stand

Status: Extant

Current stadium: The Hive

The settlement at Underhill first grew up at a confluence of several old lanes, where Silver Crispin rebuilt a cottage alehouse as the Red Lion in the mid-18th century. Underhill stadium was the home of Barnet football club from 1907 to 2013. The departure of Barnet led to a decline in trade at the Old Red Lion and the pub was sold for housing development in 2015.

The club's origins are slightly complicated. It originally formed in 1888, but before that had been known as both Woodville FC and later New Barnet FC. Known then as 'The Hillmen', their first ground was in New Barnet, before moving to Queen's Road in 1889. However, after just over a decade of relative success, Barnet FC simply dissolved in 1902 and was no more.

The journey to becoming the Barnet that play today is just as complicated. In 1890, a team called Barnet Avenue were formed. They were originally strong rivals of the earlier Barnet FC, but in 1904, with the disappearance of that club, they took the name themselves. Another team named Alston Works FC was formed in 1901, but they later changed their name to Barnet Alston FC. In 1907, Barnet Alston moved to Underhill. Then in 1912, the two teams merged to form Barnet and Alston FC, changing their name once again following the First World War to just Barnet FC, becoming the team that we know to this day.

In October 1946 Underhill hosted the first-ever live television match that was broadcast on the BBC. Twenty minutes of the first half of a match against Wealdstone were shown, followed by 35 minutes of the second half before it became too dark to see.

The Underhill pitch sloped rather alarmingly from north to south but it used to slope even more until it was improved in the late 1980s. On a windy or rainy day in years gone by it was imperative to win the toss and play 'up the hill' in the first half or suffer the consequences late in the game!

Underhill had seven stands but changed very little following the mid 1960s. Originally the terraces were constructed of steps cut into compressed cinder and earth banking with wooden sleepers. The stands were only given compass-point names around 1990.

On the bottom end of the ground was the South Stand. It was formerly known as The Bottom Goal or The West Bank and considered as a 'spiritual home' for Barnet supporters. Originally it had a short, narrow, rickety, ornate wooden roof which ran from the corner flag to the six-yard box. The terrace was then concreted and a new steel roof added in the early 1960s. The 1,016-seater South Stand which replaced it was opened in 2008 and it complied with new ground regulations. The stand was not fully finished when initially passed fit for use for spectators before an FA Cup game against Swindon Town just a matter of weeks after work had started. Building work still continued after that to fit out the interior of the stand. The stand had seats decorated with club colours amber and black.

The North Terrace, 1997.

To the left of the South Stand was the Main Stand. The first Main Stand was a wooden structure which housed some very small changing rooms when the stadium opened in 1907. It was rebuilt in 1964 at a cost of £30,000, not an insignificant sum at the time. The funding was provided by way of an interest-free loan from Barnet Urban District Council, repayable at £1,000 per year over 30 years. The new stand straddled the halfway line and had seating for around 900. This structure housed the changing rooms together with The Silver Suite and, at ground level, the Tannoy room.

Flanking the Main Stand to its right was the all-seater Family Stand, a fully covered converted terrace for both home and away supporters and was located close to the old social club.

To the left was the uncovered North West Terrace. Many Barnet fans referred to this area as The Moon as it seemed to lack any atmosphere!

Opposite the Main Stand was the East Terrace, split into three sections. This area, formerly known as The Popular Side, was finally fully upgraded in the 1960s with new roof additions either side of the raised centre section which held the television cameras. The home fans were allocated the two southernmost parts and the remaining section allocated to away supporters.

At the top end of the stadium was the North Terrace formerly known as The Top Goal. This was the smallest area of the ground and was very narrow at one end as it ran parallel with the residential Westcombe Drive gardens behind it. Regulars on this terrace have witnessed the changing appearance of occupants' flowerbeds, and the addition of sheds or patios over the years! The homeowners also got a view of the game. The crowd were separated from joining in with family Bar-B-Qs by a tall mesh fence, which also helped prevent the wildest shots from going into garden fishponds.

Alongside the North Terrace was a small section of covered seating (240) reserved for away fans. Sometimes known as the North East Family Stand,

it was of a temporary nature but was very popular with visiting fans. In the south-west corner of the ground stood the Durham Suite, named after Barnet midfielder Kevin Durham who died in 1991. The final additions to the ground were new floodlight pylons which were erected during the summer of 2010. The original floodlighting system, although modernised occasionally, had been in place for over 45 years.

Barnet were always a considerable non-league force and were champions of the Conference in 1990–91, being promoted to the old Fourth Division. In the years leading up to the beginning of the Millennium, they went on to consolidate their place in Division Three. But in the 2000–01 season, 25 losses meant that they sank back to the Conference, ending their 10-year stretch as a Football League side.

An on-going battle with Barnet Council was also at the forefront of the club's thoughts, with plans for a new stadium at South Underhill being rejected due to green belt issues, threatening the existence of the club. In 2002–03 problems persisted with the council with revised plans for the new stadium at South Underhill being rejected once again. Barnet were

promoted back again to the Football League in 2005.

Following this long dispute over Underhill, the club's chairman decided it was time for Barnet to move, especially after Barnet Council awarded Saracens RFC the Barnet Copthall (now Allianz Park) site. Barnet were relegated back to the Conference in 2013 and played their final home match at Underhill that season before moving out after 106 years – and out of the London Borough of Barnet to play at their new home, The Hive, in neighbouring Harrow.

Nobody connected with Barnet wanted to leave Underhill, but the lack of any real support from the council made it inevitable. The Hive has cost several millions and is a superb facility, the envy of many clubs. Barnet were promoted again back to League Two in 2015, with seemingly better times ahead.

Underhill remains a vacant stadium with just the London Broncos U-19s playing rugby there. The site of the empty stadium has been purchased by the government's Education Funding Agency. Plans for Underhill to be demolished to make way for a proposed new free school (Ark Pioneer Academy) have been 'deferred' until 2018.

The East Stand, 1991.

Barrow

Address: Wilkie Road, Barrow-in-Furness, LA14 5UW

Highest attendance: 16,874 v Swansea City, 9 January 1954

First league match: Barrow 0–2 v Stockport County, 27 August 1921

Final league match: Barrow 0–3 v Brentford, 24 April 1972

Other usages: Speedway, Squash

Ground layout: Main Stand, Ray Wilkie Popular Side, Holker Street End, CrossBar End

Status: Extant

Current stadium: Holker Street (Furness Building Society Stadium)

Right: The new Main Stand in 2005.

Cumbria-based Barrow AFC moved to a former rubbish tip owned by the Furness Railway in Holker Street in 1909 on a five-year lease after eight years playing at the Strawberry Ground and, later, Ainslie Street, and have remained there ever since. The club and ground played host to league football for 51 years before an on-field slump at the beginning of the 1970s.

The first structure built at the ground was a wooden all-seater stand in 1912. By 1920 the stadium was enlarged to hold 20,000 fans after Barrow purchased the ground. By 1921, when Barrow were elected into the new Third Division North of the Football League, Holker Street had been developed into an 'excellent ground' with covered concrete terracing surrounding the three remaining sides, as well as changing rooms and turnstiles. The South Stand was then dismantled and moved to the west end, then known as the Steelworks, with a larger stand built in its place.

Thirty years later the Holker Street End was covered and its opposite counterpart replaced, providing shelter on all four sides. Buying second-hand floodlights from Arsenal in 1963 was as close as Barrow got to the big time during their league stay.

With Barrow relegated to the Fourth Division in 1970 the club was struggling financially and the decision was made to create a speedway track around the edge of the football pitch, resurrecting a sport that had briefly been hosted at Holker Street in 1930. Construction involved the demolishing of the 'Steelworks End' of the ground, which had been damaged by fire, the removal of the front rows of the other terraces and a re-positioning of the pitch. Football matches had to be played with grass on top of boards which covered the speedway track, resulting in complaints from visiting teams.

Such problems were seemingly influential in the decision of the Football League clubs to vote against

Barrow when the team had to seek re-election to the league following a bottom-four finish in the Fourth Division at the end of the 1971–72 season. Barrow were demoted to the Northern Premier League. As it was, the speedway team Barrow Bombers who operated from Holker Street did so for only two years from 1972 until 1974, when the track was removed due to its unpopularity amongst other football clubs.

Following demotion and the speedway era, Holker Street became rather dilapidated. The remaining stands were demolished due to health and safety concerns, though a cover was retained for the Popular Side and terracing was pushed closer to the pitch following the removal of the speedway track.

The CrossBar leisure club (including squash courts) and bar was subsequently built at the former Steelworks End as part of a job creation scheme. This remains a dominant feature of the ground and is now the matchday hospitality suite and the club's offices. The end is only partially used by spectators. The other major development since the 1970s has been the construction of an all-seater Main Stand on the Wilkie Road side of the ground. It is situated on the halfway line with 'Barrow' picked out across the seats. The Holker Street End is now an uncovered terrace, and the area is the traditional home end, but is partially reserved for away supporters.

In 1995 the club was purchased by Stephen Vaughan, who put money into the club, allowing the building of the all-seater Main Stand. Vaughan was investigated for money laundering although no charges were ever brought. He left the club at the end of 1998, withdrawing his financial support that had been keeping it afloat.

It transpired that the Holker Street ground had been sold by Vaughan for £410,000. In 1999 the club were the subject of a compulsory winding up order and a liquidator was appointed to run the club whilst trying to establish who the legal owner of the ground was.

A new members company was formed providing financial support and with the long-term intention of taking over the running of the club. The legal disputes over the ownership of Holker Street were finally resolved in August 2002 and the new members company bought the stadium from the liquidator. In 2003 the Football Association finally allowed the 'football membership' to be transferred to the new company.

Barrow were purchased by Dallas-based businessman Paul Casson for £600,000 in September 2014. In 2015 he revealed his intention to give Holker Street a complete makeover and the current thinking is to carry out a phased plan which will result in each side of the ground eventually being redeveloped.

After dropping down the non-league pyramid, a return to the Vanarama National League has brought renewed hope that Holker Street could once again host league football in the not too distant future.

The Popular Side, September 1964.

The Holker Street End in the 1970s.

Bolton Wanderers

Burnden Park

Address: Manchester Road, Bolton, Lancashire BL3 2QS

Highest attendance: 69,912 v Manchester City, 18 February 1933

First league match: Bolton 3-1 v Everton, 14 September 1895

Final league match: Bolton 4-1 v Charlton Athletic, 25 April 1997

Other usages: FA Cup Final replay (1901), Rugby League finals

Ground layout: Manchester Road Stand (Main Stand), Great Lever End (South Stand), Burnden Stand (Darcy Lever Stand), Railway End

Status: Demolished

Current stadium: Macron Stadium

Right: The Main Stand, December 1974.

Opposite above: The Railway End, 1989, after selling part of the stand to a supermarket chain.

Opposite below: The South Stand, September 1969 – the Great Lever End.

Prior to its demolition in 1999, Burnden Park was home to Bolton Wanderers for over 100 years. From the halcyon days of the 1930s through to the 1960s, and to the leaner periods of lower-division football, the stadium saw it all.

After a period of 'wandering' around different grounds, and a 15-year residency at Pike's Lane, Bolton's first visitors to Burnden Park in 1895 were Preston North End in a friendly. Being founder members of the Football League, Wanderers had already been playing for seven years. The construction of Burnden Park for £4,000 on open land in the south-east area of the town was financed by a share issue that turned Bolton into a limited company. Wanderers had initially leased the land for £130 per annum.

Just six years later the stadium would play host to an FA Cup final replay between Tottenham Hotspur and Sheffield United.

If that was a high point, the low point in the history of both club and ground was definitely the 'Burnden Park Disaster' in March 1946, in which 33 spectators were killed and 400 injured at the Railway End owing to overcrowding. Over 65,000 fans had crammed into the stadium to witness Bolton play Stanley Matthews' Stoke City in an FA Cup quarter-final, but tragedy struck as the game kicked off, with scenes that would become all too familiar just over 40 years later at Hillsborough.

The Manchester Road (Main Stand) was built in 1905 and in 1915 an additional angled wing was added to the stand to the southern end (towards the Great Lever Terrace). The stand had a small paddock to its front, with a larger raised seating area behind. The stand housed the dressing rooms and team tunnel, and had a 'pigeon loft' type gantry on its roof.

This stand was the subject of the famous 1953 painting by artist L. S. Lowry, called *Going to the Match*. It shows part of the rear of the Manchester Road. The original painting

was sold at auction in 1999 for £1.9 million. It was bought by the Professional Footballers Association, who then lent it out to the Lowry Centre in Salford. The picture was originally entitled *Football Ground* before being renamed.

A year later in 1906, the Great Lever End was terraced and covered. Named after the local Great Lever area of Bolton, it was built by local businessman John Booth whose company also built the Manchester Road Stand, as well as erecting most of the steelwork for the new Wembley Stadium in 1923. In 1979 the stand had 4,342 seats installed on the existing terrace.

Two FA Cup final wins after the First World War enabled Bolton to replace the originally named Darcy Lever Stand with the new Burnden Stand in 1928 seating 2,750 people. This stand, as well as the ground itself, took its name from the local Burnden area of Bolton. It had a large terraced paddock area at the front, with over 2,500 seats installed in a raised area at the back.

The Railway End gained its name from the railway line that used to run across the embankment at the back of the terrace. In a scene from the 1950s comedy film *Love Match*, the football-mad locomotive driver played by Arthur Askey is seen stopping his train so he can watch the match being played on Burnden Park below.

Other than the construction of floodlighting, first used on 14 October 1957 in a friendly against Hearts, Burnden Park had now assumed the form it would take for the next 70 years.

The 1980s and early 1990s saw a lull at Burnden Park; Bolton were playing Second and Third Division football and attendances that once topped 60,000 now barely reached 20,000, due in no small part to half of the Railway End Stand being sold to a supermarket chain and torn down in 1986, spoiling the overall view of the ground.

But an upwardly mobile club such as Bolton would not languish for long, and the realisation of their ambitions required a stadium to match. The move

took place in 1997, bringing to an end 102 years of football at Burnden Park.

Bolton's last season at Burnden Park was arguably their most successful. They were promoted to the Premier League as champions in 1997 and comfortably beat Charlton 4–1 in their last game before moving to the purpose-built 28,000-capacity Reebok Stadium six miles away at the Middlebrook development. The Reebok was renamed the Macron Stadium in 2014.

The Burnden Park ground fell into disrepair with travellers occupying the car park. The ground was not demolished for two years, but then in 1999 a retail shopping park, including a large supermarket store, was constructed on the site. There is now nothing notable to see of the former football ground, although the supermarket does display a number of images of the ground and the games played there.

Bolton have witnessed two recent relegations but have been promoted back to the Championship as League One runners-up in 2016–17.

Boston United

Address: York Street, Boston, Lincolnshire PE21 6JN

Highest attendance: 11,000 v Derby County, 9 January 1974

First league match: Boston United 2-2 v Bournemouth, 10 August 2002

Final league match: Boston United 1-1 v Torquay United, 28 April 2007

Other usages: Community use, displays

International matches: England U-18 schoolboys

Ground layout: Main Stand, York Street Stand, Spayne Road Terrace, Town End/ Jakemans Stand

Status: Extant

Current stadium: York Street (Jakemans Stadium)

Right: Main Stand, 1989.

An unmistakably British-sounding stadium for a team that sounds as if it's from across the Atlantic, York Street has housed Boston United since 1933, though former club custodians insisted the site has been in use by various Boston teams since the 1880s.

The stadium has endured a number of name changes throughout the years; prior to United's formation it was known as Main Ridge, changing to Shodfriars Lane before becoming York Street. In 2009 it succumbed to taking the name of a sponsor, becoming the Jakemans Stadium.

In the mid-1950s the York Street Stand was built, and the ground's first floodlights were installed. These were first played under in 1955, when over 9,000 fans watched Boston's game against Corby Town. The new floodlights, erected in each of the four corners of the ground, allowed the Pilgrims to play in various floodlit competitions.

In 1977, Boston received a huge body blow when Football League inspectors deemed the ground unsuitable for the Football League, and although United were Northern Premier League champions yet again, runners-up Wigan Athletic were put forward instead and were elected.

The club's directors unanimously agreed that this must never happen again, and so commenced the vast undertaking of rebuilding virtually the whole of the York Street Ground, launching new fundraising schemes in 1978. The local population backed them incredibly well, and new floodlights, stands, toilets, turnstiles, terracing and snack-bars turned York Street into the ground it now is.

The Main Stand runs the length of the pitch on the north side, and has been named the Fantasy Island Stand and Staffsmart Stand for sponsorship reasons.

Opposite is the Spayne Road Terrace, a covered terrace generally considered the most atmospheric.

Behind the west goal is the Town End Terrace, now named the Jakemans Stand. Formerly for away fans, it was revered so much by Boston fans that they forced travelling supporters to a section of the York Street Stand, the oldest stand in the ground, opposite the other goal on the east side. This stand has also been known as the Benton Brothers Stand or the Lincolnshire Co-operative Stand.

Boston's brief five-year stay in the league was not without incident, York Street becoming the stamping ground of a former England player, Paul Gascoigne. Though Gazza only played five games for the club, he still evoked a positive response from the York Street faithful.

The Pilgrims' brief tenure in the Football League ended in 2007 when the team was relegated and they then unceremoniously dropped a further two divisions as a punishment for entering administration. Yet Boston United and their York Street ground ultimately survived, both harbouring the hope of league football once more. Boston still remain in the sixth-tier National League North.

Boston United, however, does not own their current Stadium at York Street, but owns the stands and has a lease that will expire in January 2018. The owners, the Malkinsons family, are seemingly not going to renew the lease. Irrespective of the lease expiring, York Street is ageing and no longer fit for purpose as a modern-day stadium. It is lacking in amenities and business opportunities, has high maintenance costs and struggles to conform to current safety standards.

Plans for a new 5,000 capacity multi-facility community stadium located south-west of the town were approved by the council in 2015, and the club have commenced with the building. Works are expected to be completed in the autumn of 2017 when Boston United will finally leave their home after 84 years.

Town End – Jakemans Stand, 1989.

Spayne Road Terrace, 1989.

Highest attendance: 34,429 v Leeds United, 25 December 1931

First league match: Bradford Park Avenue 1-0 v Hull City, 1 September 1908

Final league match: Bradford Park Avenue 0-5 v Scunthorpe United, 4 April 1970

International matches: England v Ireland (1909)

Other usages: Cricket: Yorkshire (until 1996), Bowling, Rugby (until 1907)

Ground layout: Main Stand, Low Stand, Canterbury Avenue End, Horton Park End

Status: Demolished

Current stadium: Horsfall Stadium

Right: The Low Stand, late 1970s.

Below: The Horton Park End in the early 1970s.

Park Avenue was so special to its inhabitants that they adopted its name. Bradford Park Avenue played league football at the ground for 62 years from 1908 to 1970. But even the sale of the ground three years later could not stop the club from going to the wall in 1974.

Bradford FC began playing association football in 1895, alternating home Saturdays at Park Avenue with the rugby games. When the association game was introduced to Park Avenue, facilities for spectators bore little resemblance to those of later years. The terraces were probably little more than earth banks, perhaps strengthened by railway sleepers. The initial football team was not a success.

Despite the failure of this early experiment, association football success elsewhere prompted the club to abandon rugby in 1907 and apply to join the Football League. They were not accepted; instead strangely they joined the Southern League.

Despite being newly formed, Bradford signalled their intentions by commissioning Archibald Leitch to design their home at a cost of around £10,000. It sat adjacent to Bradford Park Avenue cricket ground and upon completion could accommodate 37,000 and was considered superior to more successful neighbours City's Valley Parade.

A new enlarged 360ft-long steel pavilion (Main Stand) was erected between the football ground and cricket pitch. This included the provision of 4,000 seats on the football side plus a handful on the cricket side. This was a trademark Leitch double-decker stand, the first ground to feature it, with his typical balcony detailing.

There were three gables on each side, two at the ends and one in the centre with a clock on the cricket side and huge golden 'BFC' letters on the football side. The two end gables featured the shield from the Bradford coat of arms. The roof was covered in Welsh slate. This stand ran up to the ground's most distinctive feature, a pavilion known as the Dolls House; this was similar to Craven Cottage at Fulham, and was situated in the corner of the ground next to the goal-side uncovered terracing. This housed

dressing rooms, baths, a referee's room, refreshment facilities and a committee room.

A covered Low Stand had been built on the Park Avenue side to the west around 1900 and large uncovered concrete terraces were built behind the two goals, the Horton Park End eventually getting a roof after the Second World War. The Canterbury Avenue End remained open to the elements until the ground closed in 1973.

In 1908 Bradford FC was elected to the Second Division of the Football League. The club was promoted to the First Division in 1914 after finishing second. An opening-day 2–1 home defeat to champions Blackburn Rovers would not set the tone for a season, for Park Avenue finished in ninth place, their highest finish, five points behind table-toppers Everton.

After the First World War the club began a steady decline, relegated to the Second Division in 1921 and to the Third Division North in 1922. The rest of their existence was spent alternating between the Third and Fourth Divisions, increasingly struggling against the strong rugby influence in the area. Park Avenue remained largely unaltered, but a social club was built on part of the Canterbury Avenue terrace in the early 1970s. After several difficult playing seasons, they were finally replaced in the Football League by Cambridge United in 1970.

The club joined the Northern Premier League, selling Park Avenue in 1973 for financial reasons and sharing facilities with neighbours Bradford City. Bradford Park Avenue went into liquidation on 3 May 1974 with significant debts and folded, re-forming as a Sunday league side.

Park Avenue fell into disrepair and Leitch's stands and dressing rooms were finally demolished in 1980, but the playing field and crumbling terraces remained. The Sunday incarnation of Park Avenue returned to play a season of fixtures there in 1987 after the pitch had been cleared of debris and vegetation and made playable again. However, an indoor cricket centre was eventually erected on part of the pitch, signalling the end. The quiet neighbour had taken over.

A Saturday football side was formed in 1988 and eventually merged with the Sunday side around 1994. In 1995 Bradford Park Avenue won the North West Counties League, re-joining the Northern Premier League and moving to the Horsfall Stadium just a mile from the old Park Avenue ground. The re-formed Bradford Park Avenue play in the sixth-tier Vanarama National League North at the 3,500 capacity stadium.

Today, Park Avenue is still a cricket ground and is used by Bradford College Cricket Academy. Only a perimeter wall of the football ground remains and some of the bricked up terrace entrances can still be seen on Canterbury Avenue with admission signs still in place. However, dusty reminders of the old ground remain, albeit increasingly crept upon by the surrounding forest.

A first archaeological excavation of a goalmouth and goalpost at the ground in November 2013 by artist Neville Gabie working alongside Jason Wood, a specialist in Roman history, called the ground an extraordinarily interesting Victorian sports complex which had cricket, football, bowling, and rugby league.

He added: 'The football ground is gone and the stand is all torn down, but actually the terrace behind the goal, the old Horton Park terrace, apart from the fact that they've cut all the roof down and all the crush barriers bar one, is absolutely intact underneath the trees; it's quite extraordinary – it's a bit like a Mayan ruin.'

The Main Stand during an FA Cup match, 1967.

Brighton & Hove Albion · Goldstone Ground

Address: Newton Road, Hove, Sussex BN3 7DE

Highest attendance: 36,747 v Fulham, 27 December 1958

First league match: Brighton & Hove Albion 0–0 v Merthyr Town, 1 September 1920

Final league match: Brighton & Hove Albion 1–0 v Doncaster Rovers, 26 April 1997

Other usages: Olympic Games: football (1948), Wimbledon (European football 1995)

Ground layout: North Stand, South Stand, East Stand, West Stand

Status: Demolished

Current stadium: Falmer Stadium (American Express Community Stadium)

Right: The East Terrace, 1978.

Brighton's recent history has been characterised by the club's lack of a permanent home since they vacated the Goldstone Ground in 1997 after a near 100-year residency. The Goldstone Ground stood on Old Shoreham Road, Hove, opposite Hove Park in a partly residential area. The area was previously part of Goldstone Farm and was first used for a football match by Hove FC on 7 September 1901, a rudimentary covered West Stand for 400 spectators with turnstiles and changing rooms were already in place. Brighton & Hove Albion at this time were in the Southern League using the County Cricket Ground.

When the cricket ground became unavailable, they approached Hove to play a match at the Goldstone. Hove agreed and for the following season they began a ground-share arrangement as it made the Goldstone a commercially viable proposition.

In April 1904, Hove FC opted for a return to Hove Recreation Ground leaving Albion to sign a seven-year lease from a Mr Clark as sole tenants of the ground for £250 per year.

The club's board of directors began making improvements to the ground. In 1910 a wooden stand was purchased and was erected behind the south goal. It came from Preston Park where an agricultural show had been staged. Stretching the length of the goal-line, it seated 1,800 spectators. To the north of

the West Stand were several hundred open-air bench seats. The east banking was also improved and new turnstiles and entrances were built.

During the First World War, a rifle range was built on the ground. A number of representative rugby union matches were played to generate funds for wartime relief. By the time the war was over, the Goldstone Ground was in a terrible state. A supporters' meeting at Hove Town Hall carried a motion for renovation and £1,974 was raised. The South Stand was virtually rebuilt, the West Stand was partly re-seated, and the small terraces then existing were re-modelled.

In 1920, after the club had been elected to the Football League, the West Stand was extended northward to provide cover for another 300 seats, with new dressing-rooms, offices and a boardroom also installed at a total cost of £720. In 1926, after several years of negotiations, Brighton reached agreement for the purchase of the remaining five years of the lease. The club signed a 99-year lease with the Stanford estate, with an option to purchase the freehold outright during the next eight years. The lease contained the proviso that no structure should be built at the east end that might obstruct the view from Mr Clark's house.

In 1930 further works were carried out on the West Stand and more terracing was added to the top of the East Bank and behind the north goal. The latter works preceded the construction of the first North Stand, a simple roof covering the rear part of the terrace and about three-quarters of its width. Inaugurated in January 1931, the stand cost £1,325 which was wholly met by the supporters' club over a number of years.

The Goldstone suffered bomb damage in the summer of 1942 when a German bomb exploded at the western end of the North Stand, severely damaging the roof and girders. The roof had to be removed completely, but was replaced by the time league football returned in 1946. The blast also blew out four windows in the West Stand and covered the pitch with debris.

With ever increasing crowds, the Board decided to announce plans of a £100,000 scheme to reconstruct the ground over the following decade. The first phase was the re-modelling of the terraces. The southern third of the naturally sloping East Terrace was rebuilt and combined with the 'Chicken Run' during 1949 to create a new east enclosure, while new turnstiles and toilets were added all around the ground. The north-west corner was raised to accommodate an extra 2,000 spectators. The terracing of all standing areas was finally achieved in 1953.

The old South Stand was lifted onto foundations laid behind new terracing during the summer of 1949, an operation financed by the sale of a promising young Albion player. Five years later, the South Stand was completely rebuilt using the new foundations, but continued to serve standing spectators only.

During the 1956–57 season the North Stand was extended to the full width of the pitch. The day after Albion won the Third Division South championship in April 1958, the old West Stand was torn down, and the central third (or northern half, as it turned out because of the cost involved) of the present West Stand was erected in its place. 1961 saw the installation of floodlights at a cost of £13,523.

The West Stand.

Brighton and the Goldstone saw First Division football for four seasons between 1979 and 1983 and played host to some FA Cup triumphs on the way to Brighton's first and only FA Cup final appearance, including a 4–0 demolition of Manchester City and quarter-final victory over Norwich City. To seat the ever-increasing support, a temporary West Stand extension, nicknamed The Lego Stand, was erected in 1978 and provided 980 seats but this was dismantled six years later and sold to Worthing FC. In 1986 a family area was opened and a roof was added for the disabled area.

The South Stand became an all-seated stand in 1980 after being damaged by fire. That same summer, the old North Stand was demolished after being declared unsafe. It was upgraded with a new roof supported by four pillars, but also still served standing spectators only.

That was the summit for the Goldstone, the club being relegated from the old First Division that same 1983 cup final season, and the years that followed saw mismanagement on and off the pitch as the club slipped down the divisions and deeper into debt with the stadium increasingly beginning to decay. Wimbledon, having left Plough Lane, played their European matches at the ground in 1995.

With the club facing bankruptcy, the Goldstone was sold to developers that same year without consulting the fans. There was also the discovery that Chairman Bill Archer had changed the club's constitution to allow him and his fellow investors to profit from the sale of the ground, a move that was blocked by the FA.

The chairman endured over a year's worth of protests, the boiling point being reached at the game against York City in 1996, abandoned following a pitch invasion. Brighton were granted a temporary stay of execution, but a year later they were forced to leave, the final game at the Goldstone having the added importance of being crucial to Football League survival. They beat Doncaster Rovers 1–0

to set up a relegation decider at Edgar Street with Hereford United on the final day, which ended in a 1–1 draw, sending the Bulls down on goals scored.

The real problem was that Brighton had no new stadium at all to move to, Brighton Council rejecting plans for a new ground at Waterhall funded by the profits from a leisure development at Patcham Court Farm. A lifelong fan named Dick Knight took control of the club in 1997, having led the fan pressure to oust the previous board following their sale of the club's ground.

A ground-share with Portsmouth at Fratton Park failed to materialise, forcing Brighton to lodge 70 miles away with Gillingham between 1997 and 1999 and then 'temporarily' at the inappropriate Withdean athletic stadium, a short-term arrangement that lasted for 12 years! After planning delays, construction commenced on a new purpose-built ground at Falmer in 2008, and Brighton moved into their new home in 2011.

The Goldstone was demolished and is now a retail outlet park, characterised by a row of warehouse-style retail shops along with a drive-through fast food outlet, with little or no memorial to show eager shoppers what used to be. Brighton played in the Championship in 2016–17 and an excellent season was rewarded with automatic promotion back to the Premier League after an absence of 34 years.

Withdean Stadium – see page 154.

Brighton & Hove Albion's North Stand in the 1960s.

Bristol Rovers

Eastville Stadium

Highest attendance: 38,472 v Preston North End, 30 January 1960

First league match: Bristol Rovers 3-2 v Newport County, 1 September 1920

Final league match: Bristol Rovers 1-1 v Chesterfield, 26 April 1986

Other usages: Greyhound Racing, Speedway, American Football (1986)

Ground layout: North Stand, South Stand, Tote End, East Terrace

Status: Demolished

Current stadium: Memorial Stadium

Also known as Bristol Stadium and Bristol Stadium – Eastville, Eastville Stadium's close proximity to the Stapleton Gasworks gave Bristol Rovers fans the nickname 'Gasheads'. The River Frome which ran by the back of the South Stand was, on its day, quite odorous too. The club's time there had its explosive moments, but over the years it became clear that the location as it stood was far from satisfactory for a football stadium. Hosting League football for 66 years following election to the Football League in 1920, Eastville saw Rovers win over half their 1,279 games in front of their loyal fans, before financial difficulties forced them to move out.

The club purchased the ground in 1921, and in 1924 the South Stand comprising mostly wood was built. Greyhound racing commenced on Saturday 16 June 1928. The hub of activity for die-hard Rovers fans was the curved Stapleton Road End, behind which was the gasworks. The large covered terrace behind one of the goals built in 1935 was known as the Tote End or simply the Tote owing to the large Totaliser betting display for the greyhound racing, which would have a large effect on the club's history. The Totaliser clocks were mounted firstly at the back of the terrace and then, after a larger roof covering most of the terrace was added in 1961, on the roof fascia, giving the stand its name. The Totaliser was finally replaced by advertising in 1982.

The dog racing did well through the 1930s securing the future of the stadium, and this was in sharp contrast to the football club who were in financial difficulties. During 1939, Bristol Rovers negotiated a sale price to the Bristol Greyhound Company, albeit by the chairman, who carried out the deal without the knowledge of his fellow directors.

Eastville changed hands for £12,000 for the freehold even though its value was nearer £20,000.

The Tote End, 1976, showing the Totaliser. The referee is the infamous Clive Thomas.

£1 million worth of damage, with the ground being described as just a shell.

After playing a few games at Bristol City's Ashton Gate, Rovers temporarily moved to Bath City's Twerton Park in 1986. The move saved the club an annual cost of £30,000 plus expenses, but the historic decision to leave the club's spiritual home was regretted by many. Shortly after Rovers left Eastville the Tote End was bulldozed, and the ground became increasingly neglected.

Greyhound racing continued in their absence, but the stadium was shut down permanently on 27 October 1997. The company, now known as the BS Group, sold Eastville for development. Plans were announced for a new Bristol greyhound stadium, but these never came to fruition. The entire greyhound operation moved to sister track Swindon.

The stadium was demolished in 1998, and in 1999 a furniture superstore was erected on the site, retaining a solitary floodlight as a tribute to the old stadium. Eventually in 2015, the store informed Rovers that the floodlight was becoming unsafe and needed to be dismantled and a ceremony to remove it took place on a cold December day. After their 'temporary' absence of 10 years, Rovers returned to Bristol in 1996, taking up residence at Bristol Rugby Club's 12,000-capacity Memorial Stadium sharing the ground and eventually buying the freehold.

In 2011, the club began exploring different options with regards to the future of the club's stadium and the club announced its intention to relocate the club to a new 21,700 all-seater stadium, to be built on land at the University of the West of England's campus. To fund the project, the current site of the Memorial Stadium would be sold to a supermarket.

In September 2012, planning permission for the proposed UWE Stadium was granted by South Gloucestershire Council. In January 2013, subsequent planning permission was granted by

Rovers were granted a lease on 8 March 1940 at £400 per year to continue playing on the ground for a further 21 years. Further financial assistance saw the club come under the company's control briefly in 1945.

In 1959 the North Stand was opened, and floodlights were also installed. Eastville's record attendance occurred the following year. Another unique feature of Eastville at this time was the rosebushes and flower beds behind each goal. The large curved east terrace remained open to the elements.

The racing of dogs was not the only other sport to be seen at Eastville. It hosted a wide variety of events over the following years including motorcycle speedway which was introduced to the ground in 1977. The ground also developed a thriving Sunday market.

With the building of the M32 motorway, which encroached on the stadium, it was only a matter of time before Rovers had to find a new home, but money was not readily available. In August 1980, a fire gutted the South Stand, destroying the club's offices and changing rooms and causing more than

Bristol City Council for the building of a supermarket on the site of the Memorial Stadium. However, local and legal disputes have so far delayed the development.

Rovers were relegated at the end of the 2013–14 season, which saw the team demoted to the Conference for the first time. They returned to the Football League at the end of that first season following a victory over Grimsby Town in the play-off final. In their first season back, Rovers were promoted back to League One where they currently reside.

One cannot help but get a little wistful at what might have been. The old ground had first class motorway links, was close to major bus routes, was a few hundred yards from a railway station, and not far from the city centre. Eastville Stadium could have been huge too. Whilst the stadium was dilapidated, the site of the ground and surrounding area was ripe for redevelopment.

Twerton Park – see page 155.

Opposite: Bristol Rovers' South Stand.

Above right: The North Stand, 1988.

Right: The East Terrace, 1990, abandoned after Rovers' departure.

Burton Albion

Eton Park

Address: Princess Way, Burton upon Trent, Staffordshire DE13

Other usages: Pop concert

Ground layout: Main Stand, Popular Terrace, Brook End, Gordon Bray Stand

Status: Demolished

Current stadium: Pirelli Stadium

Eton Park was a football stadium located in Burton upon Trent. It was the home ground of Burton Albion FC from 1958 to 2005. The Brewers moved to the ground on 20 September 1958, coinciding with their promotion to the Southern League.

The formation of Burton Albion Football Club at a public meeting on 5 July 1950 brought senior football back to the town of Burton upon Trent after a 10-year absence. In the pre-war years Burton could proudly lay claim to three Football League sides: Burton Wanderers, Burton Swifts and Burton United. When a fourth, Burton Town, ceased to exist it left a void to be filled and the Brewers aimed to fill that gap.

Making use of the Wellington Street ground owned by Lloyds Foundry the club began life in the Birmingham League, making their bow on 19 August 1950 against Gloucester City in front of more than 5,000 supporters, barely a month after being formed. The Brewers spent eight years in the Birmingham League and, apart from the first and last seasons in that division, top half finishes were secured each year.

In 1958 the Brewers took the next stage in their development with the switch to the Southern League and also a move from Wellington Street to a site off Derby Road on the opposite side of the town. The supporters' club stumped up £2,000 for the land and the club spent £6,000 constructing a 300-seater stand at what would become Eton Park. The club initially struggled in the Southern League, finishing bottom in their first season and generally struggling in the lower reaches.

Another geographical alignment of the feeder leagues saw Albion return to the Northern Premier (UniBond) League in 2001 but this time it was only a one-season stay as Nigel Clough's team swept all before them winning the first league championship in the club's 52-year history in style. A league record number of points were gained, over 100 goals scored and just 30 conceded as Albion at last achieved their goal of Conference football.

The Main Stand, 1994.

The first three years in the Conference were all played at Eton Park and saw the club finish in the bottom half in each campaign as it became clear that the only way for the club to truly progress was to move away from their charismatic home of 47 years.

A great deal of money, almost £1 million, had been spent on the old ground but there was only scope for so much, and the ground still looked dated and rather shabby. A significant amount of housing development had sprung up around Eton Park too; the ground was hemmed in on two sides limiting expansion and the club had issues with neighbours over noise and light pollution.

On one side was the Main Stand, an interesting structure raised from the ground, which was all seater, and only ran for about a third of the pitch, being centred just off the halfway line. There were limited spectator facilities either side of the stand open to the elements. On the opposite side was the Popular Terrace, a small stand that didn't have any crush barriers, only a large number of posts and a basic roof.

Behind one goal was the Brook End, very similar in construction to the Popular Terrace; it also had no barriers and just sparse slab-like terracing resembling surplus pavements. It had a rudimentary corrugated roof over the terracing, supported by multiple pillars.

At the other end was another terrace, the Gordon Bray Stand, which looked more modern than the other stands and had crush barriers as well as a rather imposing metal fence in its middle.

In 2003 the club agreed a deal with Pirelli, whose factory and sports grounds lay close to Eton Park. The £7.2 million Pirelli Stadium was built on Princess Way in 2005; this was the same road as the Eton Park ground, which was then demolished and developed into housing.

Burton topped the Conference League in 2008–09 and achieved promotion to the Football League for the first time. They advanced quickly and by the end of the 2015–16 season had been promoted twice. They currently ply their trade in the Championship.

The Popular Terrace, 1994.

Cardiff City

Address: Sloper Road, Cardiff CF11 8SX

Highest attendance: 57,893 v Arsenal, 22 April 1953

First league match: Cardiff City 0-0 v Clapton Orient, 30 August 1920

Final league match: Cardiff City 0-3 v Ipswich Town, 25 April 2009

International matches: Wales (Football), Wales (Rugby League)

Other usages: Club Rugby League, Boxing, Show Jumping, Basketball, Rock Concerts

Ground layout: Canton End, Grange End, Popular Bank, Grandstand

Status: Demolished

Current stadium: Cardiff City Stadium

Right: The West Stand in the 1970s.

Below: The Canton End, the North Stand, 1980s.

Ninian Park's history was cut short one year shy of its century when Cardiff moved into their brand new Cardiff City Stadium in 2009, but the ground that was built on the site of a rubbish tip and required extensive work to get a playable surface, is synonymous with many a generation's memories of the Bluebirds. Having arrived from the nearby Sophia Gardens, newly professional Cardiff named the ground in honour of Lord Ninian Crichton-Stuart, who helped secure the lease.

The stadium featured four stands: the Canton End (which became the Spar Family Stand), the Grange End (which became the John Smith's Grange End after being sponsored by the brewery), the Popular Bank (commonly known as the 'Bob Bank' as it was one shilling [5p] originally to obtain entrance) and the Grandstand.

The Canton Stand was erected upon the club's election to the Football League in 1920. Fully covered with a very high roof-

line and eventually with all seating on top of the old terrace, it was situated at the north goal end. It had several supporting poles along the width of the stand. The rear of that stand was also home to a number of executive boxes and hospitality areas, and although work on them began in the early 1980s, they were not completed until 2001 due to financial difficulties. The club's ticket office was also located within this stand.

Eight years later saw the opposite Grangetown End covered. It was officially opened on 1 September 1928 before a league match against Burnley by the Lord Mayor of Cardiff and could hold 18,000 spectators. The area behind the goal where the stand

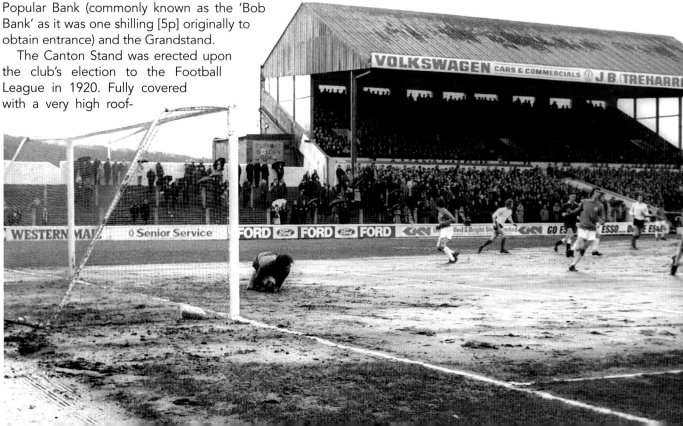

was built was previously an earth embankment. In the 1946–47 season, a spectator fell through the roof of the Grange End during a game with Bristol City. This hole remained in the Grange End roof until its demolition.

The original stand was demolished during the 1977–78 season as structural engineers deemed it to be unsafe and it was replaced by a small, uncovered concrete terrace. The John Smith's Grange End was renovated and covered in 2001 after Sam Hammam took over as chairman. The stand also had several supporting poles, and one section housed the away fans. This away section had terracing to the back and seating at the front. One nice feature of the stand was a small gable sitting on top of the roof, with a clock in its centre.

Ninian Park's modest original wooden main stand on the Sloper Road side was initially able to hold 200 seated supporters and was made of wood with a canvas roof and this unsurprisingly was destroyed by fire in January 1937, allegedly by thieves attempting to open the safe, and was replaced by a larger, more imposing brick structure a year later.

The final incarnation of the Grandstand was a two-tier, all-seater stand, with old-fashioned wooden seats in the upper tier, and modern plastic seating in the lower tier. This stand also had several supporting poles holding up the roof. The most interesting feature was the roof, which was in two parts, with a propped roof covering the upper tier, and an extension to the front which covered the lower tier. This stand also housed the area in which the player dressing rooms and tunnel were incorporated, as well as housing the dugouts, the VIP area and the press/media benches.

Opposite the Grandstand running along the touchline on the east side of the ground was the Popular Bank, referred to as the 'Bob Bank'. The Popular Bank had covered seating to the rear of the stand, and uncovered standing terrace to the front. The seating had many supportive poles, and in keeping with the tradition of many football teams,

many seats were coloured white and when viewed from above spelled the word 'CARDIFF'. An advert for Captain Morgan Rum remained on the stand roof for over 40 years. It is widely believed to be the longest-serving advert at any football ground. The stand was originally a large open embankment before the roof was constructed in 1958.

Floodlights were installed in 1960 and it was to prove a timely innovation as Ninian Park saw a number of European ties in the 1960s and 1970s, with Cardiff qualifying for the European Cup Winners Cup on several occasions by winning the Welsh Cup. The most notable tie, without doubt, was a memorable 1–0 victory over Spanish champions Real Madrid in the quarter-finals in 1971.

The Welsh national rugby league team, the Wales Dragons, used Ninian Park as one of its home venues. The ground hosted seven internationals between 1981 and 1995. Cardiff City Blue Dragons rugby league team used the ground as their home between 1981 and 1984.

Most accepted that Cardiff City's Ninian Park's old stands were in desperate need of a facelift and the ground was 'antiquated to the point of ruin'; it was a place that differed little from how it had appeared in

the 1960s and was also one of the few above League One level that still contained standing areas.

In the end it wasn't given a facelift, but was replaced entirely. Cardiff 's farewell to Ninian Park was one of heartbreak in 2008–09 when they lost 0–3 to Ipswich Town, which, coupled with a final-day loss away to Sheffield Wednesday, caused them to miss out on a play-off spot on goals scored, thanks to Preston North End's victory against Queens Park Rangers.

After the final home match, the bulldozers moved in, and the site was rapidly demolished; it is now a residential housing development with the same name. Developers built 142 new homes on the site. A planted square was proposed at the centre of the new development, in the area of Ninian Park's centre spot. The first families moved into the new housing in November 2010. Cardiff City began the following campaign at the new Cardiff City Stadium which cost an estimated £40 million. Following three consecutive play-off defeats, the stadium eventually saw Premier League football in 2013–14, but the club are now back in the Championship.

Below: The Popular Stand in the 1990s.

Chester City Sealand Road and Deva Stadium

Names: The Stadium (Sealand Road) and Deva Stadium

Addresses: (Sealand Road) Sealand Road, Chester CH1 6BS; (Deva Stadium) Bumpers Lane, Chester CH1 4LT

Highest attendances: 20,738 v Chelsea, 16 January 1952 – FA Cup (Sealand Road)

5,987 v Scarborough, 17 April 2004 (Deva Stadium)

First league matches: Chester 3-1 v Halifax, 12 September 1931 (Sealand Road)

Chester City 3-0 v Burnley, 5 September 1992 (Deva Stadium)

Final league matches: Chester City 2-0 v Rotherham United, 28 April 1990 (Sealand Road)

Chester City 1-2 v Darlington, 2 May 2009 (Deva Stadium)

Other usages: Liverpool U-21 (Deva Stadium)

Ground layout: (Sealand Road) Main Stand, Popular Side, Sealand Road End, Kop End; (Deva Stadium) North Stand, South Stand, West Stand, East (Main) Stand

Status: Demolished (Sealand Road); Extant (Deva Stadium)

Current stadium: Deva Stadium (Lookers Vauxhall Stadium)

Chester has the distinction of having two former league grounds: Sealand Road and subsequently the Deva Stadium. One lost its status through demolition, the other through the club's relegation. Chester FC (they added the City in 1983) moved to the former in 1906 from Whipcord Lane.

Chester were elected to the Lancashire Combination in 1910 and after the war were founder members of the Cheshire County League which they won three times in five years during the 1920s.

These successes, coupled with improved cover on the Main Stand, helped Chester win election to the Football League in 1931. The stadium was one of the first to have a public address system. One of Sealand Road's major problems in those early years was flooding from the nearby River Dee which occurred at every high spring tide, as the river flowed through the town centre. This was eventually solved in 1936 when the club installed a proper drainage system at a cost of £400.

Floodlights were installed in 1960, with the towering 126ft (38m) lights being used for the first time in a 2–2 League Cup draw with Leyton Orient in October of that year.

Behind the goals were the barrel-roofed Sealand Road End, nicknamed 'The Barn' by supporters, and the commonly named Kop, an open terrace made unusually from paving stones. On one side was the Popular Side covered in 1968 (half for home fans, half for away fans).

The floodlights were later updated in 1974 before the stadium played host to Chester's most famous League Cup semi-final run, taking on teams like Leeds United, Newcastle and Aston Villa.

In 1979, the look of Sealand Road was significantly changed when a new grandstand was opened, replacing the previous small stand. Towering over the rest of the ground, the 2,874-capacity stand provided improved viewing facilities, but was criticised for reducing atmosphere levels as it was detached from the rest of the stadium. This stand was sometimes referred to unofficially as the Ian Rush stand as it was his sale to Liverpool that allegedly financed it.

The ground began to decay in the 1980s and Chester suffered a major blow in August 1989, when it was announced the club had been refused a safety certificate for its away standing areas. This reduced the capacity of the stadium to below 6,000. It would be their final season there. City signed off at their home of over 80 years with a victory over Rotherham United that spared them saying farewell with relegation.

Sealand Road had been sold to property developers in 1990 owing to financial pressures, and was left derelict for three years while homeless Chester City took up temporary residence at Macclesfield Town's Moss Rose ground, 45 miles away. The stadium was demolished in 1993 in favour of a retail park, by which point Chester had moved to the newly-built £3 million Deva Stadium nearby. The main stand roof at Sealand Road was sold for use by Port Vale for their uncovered away Hamil Road End enclosure in 1992.

Named after the Roman fort and settlement that eventually became Chester, the Deva Stadium held just over 5,000 supporters and was the first to fully comply with the Taylor Report, including spaces for disabled supporters and automatic turnstiles. The modest stadium took just eight months to complete. Chester's early season league fixtures had to be re-scheduled to allow for the ground to be completed and the season started with four away games.

The stadium was located within the Sealand Road Industrial Estate and is renowned as being on the border between England and Wales, with the pitch, front gates and main office in England (Cheshire) and the rear of the west stand in Wales (Flintshire). The address of the ground is officially classed as England, due to the main entrance of the building being in England! The owners of the ground are Chester and Cheshire West council.

All the four sides are covered and are roughly the same height with each stand having Perspex windshields to each side, whilst the corners of the ground are open. The stadium has three sides seated with the home end being terraced. The Main (East)

Below: The Kop End at Sealand Road, 1990.

Left: The Main Stand, Sealand Road, 1980.

Stand is slightly taller than the facing stand, having a few more rows of seating and some enclosed glassed viewing areas at the back of it. The home north end was named the Harry McNally Terrace in 2006 after a respected former manager.

There is also the West Stand (half for home fans and half away fans) and the South Stand (away fans). The South Stand was converted from terracing to seating in the summer of 2007. The stadium is completed with a set of four thin modern floodlight pylons.

The Deva Stadium hasn't provided much luck in league football for Chester, as they were relegated to Division Three in their first season at the ground. They bounced back at the first attempt, but successive relegations in 1995 and 2000 saw them lose their Football League status. Despite making a brief return in 2004, Chester dropped back into the Conference in 2009, completing their lost league grounds brace. The club was wound up in March 2010 after succumbing to the combination of a 25-point deduction, breaches of Conference rules and financial problems. They were expelled from the Conference.

From the ashes arose Chester Football Club. The club began its inaugural season in the Northern Premier League Division One North following a successful appeal to the FA against their initial placement in the North West Counties League. The team continued to play its home games at the Deva Stadium which has had several sponsorship names.

In the club's first three seasons it was the successive league champions of the NPL Division One North (2010–11), the NPL Premier Division (2011–12), and the Conference North (2012–13). Since that time, Chester have played in the Vanarama National League, but have hopes that a return to league football is more than just a possibility.

Above right: Chester City's Deva Stadium, 1995.

Right: Chester City's Sealand Road, 1986.

Name: The Recreation Ground (Saltergate)

Address: Saltergate, Chesterfield, Derbyshire S40 4SX

Highest attendance: 30,561 v Tottenham Hotspur (FA Cup), 12 February 1938

First league match: Chesterfield 2-2 v Lincoln, 9 September 1899

Final league match: Chesterfield 2-1 v Bournemouth, 8 May 2010

Other usages: Cricket (to 1894)

Ground layout: Main Stand, Saltergate End/ Spion Kop, Compton Street Terrace/Popular Side, Cross Street Terrace

Status: Demolished

Current stadium: Proact Stadium

Right: The Popular Side/Compton Street Terrace, 1981.

Chesterfield could lay claim to being the first team to imaginatively title their home the Recreation Ground, as they were based there from 1871. Consequently regarded as one of the country's oldest football stadiums, it endured its time as a league venue with minimal change to its appearance. It is more popularly known, however, as Saltergate. The ground's record attendance listed was in the FA Cup; the Football League record of 28,268 came against Newcastle just over a decade later, but by the time of its closure the capacity had been reduced to 8,504.

Like most grounds of the time it was shared by the sports of football and cricket, but this double life ended shortly before Chesterfield's league debut at the end of the 19th century as Chesterfield Town. A wooden pavilion was developed on the eastern side of the ground later in the 1870s but otherwise it remained simply an open field during this era.

A small, uncovered grandstand with benched seating for around 400 was added in 1893.

League football came to Saltergate in 1899 with Chesterfield Town's election to play in the Second Division of the Football League. The club's step up necessitated remedial work on a pitch that sloped markedly from north to south, most notably the removal of a hill in the north-west corner, the spoil from which was dumped at the Saltergate end.

In addition, the grandstand was enlarged and roofed over, its capacity increasing to around 800 spectators. Fencing was erected on the Compton Street side to obscure the free view from adjacent back gardens, modest coverage later being added on this side. After a decade of financial struggle, with other clubs who had invested in their stadia vying for an opening in the Football League, Chesterfield Town were voted out in 1909.

In a bid to return, a running track was constructed around the ground's perimeter, said to offer up to 10,000 fans a decent view, and a white picket fence was constructed around the pitch to replace the previous wire boundary. However, any ambitions

Cross Street Terrace, 1992.

In 1936 the club borrowed around £14,000 to fund the erection of a new brick and steel Main Stand by Scottish architect Archibald Leitch. Demolition of the old wooden stand began at the close of the 1935–36 season, which again saw the club promoted to the Second Division. The official opening of the new two-tier stand came in November, with Sheffield United visiting for a league fixture and a new record crowd of 26,519. This record would be broken again two years later. With the completion of the new stand, all four sides of the ground had taken on an appearance that would still be recognisable at the time of its closure.

After the Second World War, the club faced a pressing need to raise funds to service the debt on the new stand and pay off the bank loan. Further ground development became somewhat limited as a result. In 1949, with the council rejecting plans for a move to a new ground, the club made what was to be its final major investment in the ground prior to the Millennium, engaging Leitch and Partners to renew all the ground's cinder terracing with concrete and install their patented crush barriers.

In 1957 the first set of floodlights came second-hand from Sheffield's Bramall Lane and lay rusting behind the Kop before the money and the will were found to get them up. As each one was put up, they began to twist, and the first one was erected and dismantled more than once. In the end, three were erected before the whole venture was written off as a failure, and a new set were sought.

In 1961, however, modest ground improvements were implemented after significant fundraising efforts by supporters which allowed the Saltergate Kop to be roofed in the same year. Despite acquiring new lights in 1963, boardroom prevarication meant that Saltergate was the final league ground in England to install floodlights, with Chesterfield's first home game under lights not being played until the 1967–68 season.

In 1979 the centre section of the Compton Street Terrace was re-roofed and a wooden television gantry added, the only notable ground work in the

proved short-lived and the club was forced into voluntary liquidation in 1915. A fourth club, the present Chesterfield, was established in 1919 at the instigation of the local authority. The club continued to base itself at Saltergate as league football returned to the town in 1921, when Chesterfield FC became founder members of the new Third Division North.

That year saw the first alteration of the stadium when it had to move south by 20ft to accommodate the extension of Cross Street behind it. Initial ground development left the club with a tidy Main Stand that ran some three quarters of the pitch length and

seated 1,600, a roofed Popular Side and uncovered ends. Terracing was made of cinder embankments (from the running track), with a few wooden crush barriers tamped into the dirt at random-looking intervals. A wooden hut provided dressing room accommodation at the northern end of the stand.

In 1931, at a time of growing ambition for the club, terracing was cut into the cinder banking of the Kop and further earth removal from the Cross Street to Saltergate end was undertaken to level the pitch. The Cross Street End would remain uncovered throughout.

decade. After that time, with the ground being tightly surrounded by housing that restricted development, the increasing need for a move gained momentum. The board put forward many proposals in the 1990s, almost all rejected.

In late 2000, more than 10 years after the Taylor report, the future of football at Saltergate became mired in crisis with three sides of the ground under threat of closure from the Football Licensing Authority. This was narrowly averted. These were turbulent times for the club under the chairmanship of Darren Brown, who was later jailed for fraud. The supporters put the club into administration and then began to piece it back together. One of the jobs the supporters completed was to make the Compton Street side all seater.

The stadium from then gradually began to look its age as the years passed, and a vote in 2006 saw more than 90% back a plan to switch to the site of the former Dema Glass factory, around a mile from the town centre. In 2010, after 111 years, the club moved to the new £13 million 10,000-seater B2net Stadium located in the Whittington Moor area of the town. It was renamed the Proact Stadium in 2014.

Just before the move, Saltergate featured widely in the filming of *The Damned United*, the 2009 film about Brian Clough's time at Leeds United. It was used to represent the by then demolished Baseball Ground, and was chosen as it had not undergone any major modifications since the 1970s.

In January 2012, the football club sold the Saltergate site to a nationally-profiled company to construct around 68 houses at the site. The demolition to make way for the homes began in April and was completed in July the same year. The development was named 'Spire Heights' (after 'Spireites', the Chesterfield supporters) which gave a respectful nod to the site's former users. Sadly, Chesterfield were relegated from League One at the end of the 2016–17 season after finishing in last place.

Saltergate's Main Stand, 1992.

Colchester United

Layer Road

Address: Layer Road, Colchester, Essex
CO2 7JJ

Highest attendance: 19,072 v Reading
(abandoned – fog), 27 November 1948

First league match: Colchester United
0–0 v Bristol Rovers, 19 August 1950

Final league match: Colchester United 0–1
v Stoke City, 26 April 2008

Ground layout: Main Stand,
Popular Terrace, The Clock End, Layer Road End

Status: Demolished

Current stadium: The Colchester
Community Stadium
(Weston Homes Community Stadium)

Right: The Popular Terrace, August 1969.

Layer Road was built in 1907 and has been described as everything from 'modest' to 'ramshackle', but it was the battleground for Essex side Colchester United for seven decades. Originally inhabited by rivals Colchester Town, United benefited from their dissolution in 1937 when they moved in.

The Main Stand was built in 1933 before United's arrival. The Popular Stand and the Layer Road End were also already in place. The Clock End was originally called the Spion Kop.

Just a year into United's tenancy, the Layer Road End roof was blown off by relentless winds, damaging some surrounding housing. After the war, the club returned to the ground, and the Main Stand was extended for the 1946–47 season. Soon after, the Popular Side stand was demolished and the timber used to repair and renovate the Layer Road End. The stand was a low covered terrace barely taller than the goal in front of it.

A storm claimed the roof again a decade later, but this time a steel shortage prevented an immediate restoration. So for the 1949–50 season, the stand had no roof. After their time in the Southern League, Colchester were elected to the Football League in June 1950, boasting an average gate of 8,500, an amazing achievement when, because of the War, they had only been in competition for seven full seasons.

The 1956–57 season proved to be Colchester's best finish in their history (until 2006); they went 20 league games undefeated between December 1956 and Easter 1957. During that run Colchester hosted third-placed rivals Ipswich at Layer Road, and a record league crowd of 18,559 witnessed a 0–0 draw. Over 4,000 were turned away and 120 fans watched from the Popular Side roof.

After initially shelving plans owing to cost, Layer Road was fitted with floodlights in 1959, thanks to proceeds from a lucrative FA Cup tie with Arsenal.

In 1971, Layer Road was purchased from the council with a series of covenants placed on the ground. That year saw Don Revie's mighty Leeds United humbled 3–2 by Fourth Division Colchester at Layer Road in the fifth round of the FA Cup.

By the turn of the 1980s, the club's chairman announced that Layer Road was in need of £280,000 worth of basic safety improvement to meet legislation. Plans were drawn up to remove one end altogether and construct both a 5,000-capacity stand at the Layer Road End and a new Main Stand on the Popular side. The plans never came to fruition, and further plans for an enhanced stadium were rejected by the council on the basis of the covenants.

Five years later, following the Bradford disaster, Layer Road faced a £500,000 bill for safety improvements. With the club struggling financially, coupled with low attendances, sections of the ground were closed off, reducing capacity to 4,900. Colchester dropped out of the Football League in 1990 after finishing in last place.

Layer Road was sold back to Colchester Borough Council in the early 1990s for £1.2 million to help clear the club's debts, and Colchester United leased the stadium back. Layer Road was reacquainted with league football after just two seasons, and the Clock End was covered and fitted with seats in 1996.

With the lease due to expire in 2002, a preferred council-owned site at Cuckoo Farm in Colchester was identified by consultants in 1998. Plans for the new stadium were submitted in April 1999, with planning consent approved in 2003. The council backed the £14.23 million project by taking out a £10.23 million loan in November 2006, with the remaining £4 million supplied in the form of grants from the Football Foundation and local government and development agencies. Construction began on the new site in July 2007.

By this time, Colchester had soared to the lofty heights of the Championship in 2006, but Colchester's farewell to Layer Road was in somewhat sombre circumstances as they hosted Stoke City, knowing they were heading back to League One and that their brand new Colchester Community Stadium would be hosting third-tier football. However, Colchester United could no longer be accused of having a ground not befitting league football.

Nearing its final time, the old Layer Road stadium was described as follows: the Layer Road End contained a terrace split into two halves. Both sides were of an equal height (nine rows high) and fully covered, with the section behind the goal cut out, reminiscent of Goodison Park in the 1960s. The Main Stand was split into three parts. Nearest and furthest from the 'away' end were two small terraces, both covered, whilst in the middle stood a seated section. The roof of the seated section also carried on over the far terrace, whilst the near one had its own roof, which made it appear slightly separate. Opposite was the Clock End, which was a small all-seated stand, with more rows at one end than the other. Adjacent to this was 'Barside' or Popular Side. Like the Main Stand opposite, it was split into three sections, with an uncovered terrace at the far end, a larger covered terrace in the middle, and at the Layer Road end a covered, temporary stand, which provided seating for visiting fans.

Layer Road was locked for the last time on 17 July 2008 after 98 years in use, and was demolished by the end of that year. Almost three years later, a deal was signed to build flats and houses on the site, with a central open grassed space to reflect its history as a football ground. In 2015, a bronze statue of Peter Wright (Colchester United's Player of the Century) was unveiled by his widow Lindsey and Sir Bob Russell MP to commemorate him and the fact that the site was home to Colchester United for 70 years. Colchester United currently play in League Two.

Below: The Main Stand.

Coventry City
Highfield Road

Address: King Richard Street, Coventry, West Midlands CV2 4FW

Highest attendance: 51,455 v Wolverhampton Wanderers, 29 April 1967

First league match: Coventry City 0-5 v Tottenham Hotspur, 30 August 1919

Final league match: Coventry City 6-2 v Derby County, 30 April 2005

Ground layout: Main Stand, West Stand, East Stand/Swan Lane Terrace, North Stand/ Thackhall Street Stand

Status: Demolished

Current stadium: The Ricoh Arena

Right: Swan Lane Terrace, 1967.

Coventry City spent over 100 years at Highfield Road, straddling three centuries. They arrived in 1899 after brief spells at nearby Dowells Field and Stoke Road. The stadium was frequently a site of innovation in British football, and it holds the notable distinction of being England's first all-seater stadium despite reverting back to terracing four years later.

In early 1899, with the club in the Birmingham League, preparations began for the laying out of a proper ground on land from the Craven Cricket Club. A row of elm trees was removed, the pitch levelled and a 12-row stand, holding 2,000 spectators, was built on the King Richard Street side, where the later Main Stand was situated. The total cost of the project was £100, a sum that left the club in dire straits for some time. Highfield Road had one of the largest playing surfaces in the English leagues.

In 1910 the proceeds of the first decent FA Cup run financed the construction of a new barrel-roofed Main Stand at a cost of £1,200. The club, by then in the Southern League, took the scalps of two First Division

clubs in reaching the quarter-final before losing to Everton in front of a then ground record 19,000 crowd. Coventry were elected to the Second Division of the Football League for the 1919–20 season.

In 1922 the Spion Kop (or East Terrace), described as a scarred and totally shapeless mess, was built up at the Swan Lane end of the ground using waste concrete from the relaying of the city's tram track. In 1937 the West Terrace was covered by a roof purchased for £2,200 from Twickenham Rugby ground. On the pitch, the club were relegated from the Second Division in 1925 and struggled in the Third Division for the rest of the decade.

In 1936, to celebrate City's promotion back to the Second Division and with gates regularly topping 25,000, the 'rotting planks' of the original 1899 stand were demolished to make way for a new Main Stand at a cost of £14,000. In November of that year the club purchased the freehold of the ground from the Mercers Company for £20,000, thanks to a loan from Sir John Siddeley, chairman of carmakers Armstrong-Siddeley.

The additional lattice-board standing extension to the Kop, known as the 'Crows Nest', was added in 1938, and in 1939 a canopy extension was built on to the Main Stand. Highfield Road could now accommodate over 40,000 spectators as was demonstrated on a number of occasions as the team went close to promotion to the First Division in the two seasons preceding the outbreak of war.

Amazingly, the Highfield Road stands survived the appalling air raids of November 1940, although three direct hits destroyed the pitch; but by 1942 things had been sufficiently patched up to stage matches again.

In October 1953 basic floodlights were installed on poles, and were first used for a friendly game against Queen of the South. In 1957 the originals were sold to Crewe and an improved set of lights made their debut for a game against Third Lanark. The Supporters' Club paid for the new lights at a cost of £15,000 and the pylons were still being used as late as 1991.

In November 1961 chairman Derrick Robins appointed as manager former Fulham player and chairman of the Professional Footballers Association Jimmy Hill and a transformation began. This Sky Blue era under Robins and Hill sparked a massive ground improvement programme, ably carried out by Robins' building company.

The rebirth began in 1963 with the replacement of the north Thackhall Street Stand, using innovative prefabricated units and a distinctive vaulted roof. The new 'Sky Blue Stand', which cost £120,000, was fully operational for the start of 1964–65 season as City re-entered the Second Division after a 12-year gap.

Two years later the club won promotion to the First Division for the first time in their history. Highfield Road saw a record crowd of 51,455 for the vital match against Wolves. That close season, the old covered terrace, home to the Sky Blue 'choir', was demolished and replaced by the double-decker West Stand, with 3,200 seats on top of terracing. That first season in the First Division saw large crowds at the stadium and the final average was approaching an incredible 35,000.

On 16 March 1968, the Main Stand was gutted by fire and with it the Second Division Championship Trophy and many of the club's records. The stand was rebuilt almost immediately at a cost of £150,000, and was completed in time for the start of the following season, although the first two home games were postponed. This third new stand in four years complete with restaurant and striking aluminium roof made Highfield Road arguably the most modern stadium in the land.

In 1973 defects were discovered in the roof of the Sky Blue Stand and the distinctive vaulted section was replaced by a flat roof; then, early in 1983, part of the replacement roof collapsed in gales but the damage was quickly patched up.

In 1981 the controversial decision was taken to convert Highfield Road into England's first all-seater stadium and 8,000 extra seats were installed at a cost of £400,000 reducing the capacity at a stroke from 36,500 to 20,600. This unanimously unpopular decision was intended, amongst other things, to deter hooliganism but instead it alienated the home fans.

Attendances dropped as performances on the pitch deteriorated and the failed experiment accelerated Hill's resignation as chairman. The seats were ripped out of the eastern Kop in 1985 and the terraced end partially rebuilt to allow a better view and an increased capacity.

The Sky Blues were founder members of the Premier League in 1992, and in the summer of 1993 work commenced on the new East Stand and the team played its home games to a three-sided stadium for one season whilst the new stand rose from the wreck of the flattened Kop.

The East Stand cost £4.3 million, the majority of which came from the Football Trust and the brewers Mitchell & Butlers. This, together with the new roofs on the Main Stand and Sky Blue Stand, meant that

The Main Stand in 1967 – pre-fire!

over £7 million was spent on the ground during the 1990s.

Throughout the 1990s, Highfield Road continued to host top-flight football, but after that things didn't go so well, and at the end of the 2000–01 season Coventry were relegated from the top flight after an uninterrupted stay of 33 years. However, the club retained bigger ambitions and wanted a larger stadium and after several blueprints, the new Arena design was agreed, with work commencing on the new 34,000-seater stadium in 2003.

By this time, Highfield Road lacked facilities compared to the new stadia of similar-sized clubs and was looking shabby. Apart from the cramped facilities and restricted views, another reason for relocation was that parking facilities in the local area were wholly inadequate. The Sky Blues' final season at Highfield Road was the 2004–05 Nationwide Division One season. Their last home game witnessed a 6–2 drubbing of Derby County.

City moved to their purpose-built new home, the Ricoh Arena, in 2005. Demolition work began at Highfield Road in February 2006 and was completed by the end of the following month, despite a fire. The site was used for housing development with the area of the pitch being retained and re-turfed for the residents and their children to continue the tradition of playing football on that space.

Since moving, the club and the Ricoh Arena are passing through stormy and turbulent times, including in the past ground-sharing with Northampton Town at Sixfields. Sadly, Coventry were relegated to League Two at the end of the 2016–17 season after finishing in last but one place, and the future of the club currently looks bleak and uncertain.

Above: Thackhall Street Stand, 1996.

Below: Highfield Road's re-built Main Stand.

Crawley Town   Town Mead

Address: Ifield Avenue, Crawley, Sussex
RH11 7AJ

Highest attendance: 4,104 v Barnet
(FA Cup), November 1993

Ground layout: Main Stand, North Stand,
Shed End, Firestation End

Status: Demolished

Current stadium: Broadfield Stadium
(The Checkatrade Stadium)

There are early references to Town Mead, or Town Meadow to give it its full name, when pleasure fairs were held there at the end of the 19th century, around the time the club was formed, and it was Crawley Town's home from 1949 until May 1997.

Crawley Town FC played their formative years in the West Sussex League. Five years later they entered the Mid-Sussex League and won the Senior Division in only their second season.

In 1949 the club moved from their Malthouse Farm base and relocated to Town Mead. The ground was situated on Ifield Avenue, adjacent to the West Green playing fields, just west of the town centre and adjacent to the fire station. Originally Town Meadow was just a field. The bank did not exist in 1949 and this, when built, was man made to keep the non-paying public out.

Two years after moving to Town Mead, they entered the Sussex County League before switching again five years later to the Metropolitan League, which was a competition for both professional and amateur sides. Crawley retained their amateur status and went on to win the Metropolitan League Challenge Cup in 1959.

The club became semi-professional in 1962, joining the Southern League. The 1969–70 season also saw a run to the fourth qualifying round of the FA Cup where the Reds lost 0–2 to Wimbledon in a second replay. The first replay, at Town Mead, was witnessed by an official record crowd of 3,256 (though those in attendance estimate it was more like 6,000), a record that stood for 22 years.

By its own patrons' admission, Town Mead was never the most salubrious stadium, often having the air of a 'make do and mend' facility. As late as the

Until the Cup run of 1991, there were no crush barriers in The Shed, but during the fourth qualifying round replay against Horsham, attended by a then record 3,427 fans, the wall at the front of The Shed collapsed when Crawley took an early lead so the club were forced to install two rows of barriers, plus a proper front barrier, before the club received the go-ahead to stage the first-round match against Northampton Town. As the team progressed, a record crowd of 4,104 filled Town Mead for an FA Cup tie with League One Barnet in November 1993.

The original Main Stand, a rudimentary covered area extending to around half the pitch length, was knocked down in the summer of 1994 and replaced with a modern version, complete with a Portakabin/boardroom on the roof.

The Firestation End was also just a grass bank, though some basic steps had been dug into it behind the goal. These didn't really last. This side was finally developed, firstly with a couple of rows of terracing and in the final year or two at Town Mead with a small covered terrace.

However, demand for land near the town centre was increasing, and this led to the club moving in 1997. They relocated to the new purpose-built £5 million Broadfield stadium now owned by the borough council. The first match there was a friendly against Port Vale on 24 July.

Town Mead was sold for housing, and the subsequent development bears the same name and is part of a leisure park with cinemas, bowling alley, health club, bars and restaurants.

Following their move Crawley achieved great success, being promoted to the Conference in 2004. After a very shaky period in 2006, which led to points docking and administration, Crawley Town came with an inch of liquidation before they finally survived. From then on, fortunes changed for the better, and the season 2010–11 saw Crawley Town promoted to the Football League for the first time, and the following season they were promoted again to League One. The team spent three seasons there before demotion back to League Two in 2015–16, where they currently remain.

mid-1980s, the ground was still very basic. On the southern side of the ground, backing on to Ifield Avenue, was a small wooden stand built in 1949 with wooden seats for about 250 people along with the management benches. The ground also possessed a difficult and cloying pitch which after heavy rain made good football well nigh impossible. The northern side of the ground was for many years just a grass bank with a small hut on the top of it. It was not at all ideal for spectators when it was wet.

The northern side was developed during the 1990–91 season. Initially a couple of steps of concrete and a wooden fence were added, but later the fence became corrugated plastic-coated steel and a couple more steps were added. The benches were also moved from the main stand to this side of the ground.

Behind the goal at the western end of the ground was The Shed End. This consisted of numerous very large steps of terracing that ran the full width of the pitch. The middle third or so was covered, hence 'The Shed'. The roof was damaged during the great storm in October 1987.

Dagenham and Redbridge   Victoria Road

Address: Victoria Road, Dagenham, Essex RM10 7XL

Highest attendance: 7,200 v Reading (FA Cup), 15 January 1968

First league match: Dagenham and Redbridge 2-2 v Wycombe Wanderers, 18 August 2007

Final league match: Dagenham and Redbridge 3-0 v Crawley Town, 30 April 2016

International matches: UEFA Youth International matches

Other usages: West Ham Development team

Ground layout: Carling Stand/Family Stand, North Stand, Pondfield End (Traditional Builders Stand), Bury Road End (aka the Clock End)

Status: Extant

Current stadium: Victoria Road (London Borough of Barking & Dagenham Stadium)

Dagenham Football Club was one of the four antecedent clubs of the Football League club Dagenham and Redbridge, and was formed in 1949. The other three clubs – Ilford, Leytonstone and Walthamstow Avenue – all possess heritages that date from the 19th century. Dagenham initially played at a venue called the Arena.

Victoria Road had hosted football since 1917, when the Sterling Works side, whose factory was situated alongside, used it. It was not fully enclosed until the summer of 1955, when the council acquired the freehold and the successful Briggs Sports side moved out to Rush Green Road, and Dagenham FC, given a choice of two locations, moved from the Arena to Victoria Road. An initial rental of £80 gave way to a five-year lease at £130 per annum.

During that summer the club levelled and re-seeded the pitch, and removed the stones from the playing surface. They then extended the banking and the terracing. The only cover was a tiny wooden stand on the south side of the ground, which was steep and narrow and had a few rows of seating. The Main Stand opposite was built that autumn and was opened on 7 January 1956 by the chairman of the Essex County FA. It was reported that the new stand had a capacity of 800.

During mid-season in 1956 the turnstile block at the Victoria Road side of the ground was added, and the men's toilets situated at the Victoria Road end were also built.

The first floodlit match at Victoria Road was Dagenham versus Woodford in the FA Youth Cup on 26 September 1957 and the first senior match was a friendly against Rainham Town on 19 March 1958.

In the summer of 1958 the cover over the North Side was erected at a cost of £1,400, a substantial sum in those days. This was a period of great success for the club. The attendance record was set in January 1968 with the visit of Reading in the FA Cup when 7,200 crammed into the ground.

The club continued to be successful throughout the 1970s, winning the FA Trophy in 1980. In 1981 the club were admitted to the Alliance Premier League, where they remained until finishing bottom in 1987–88, when they were relegated back to the Isthmian League.

Right: The old Main Stand, 1993.

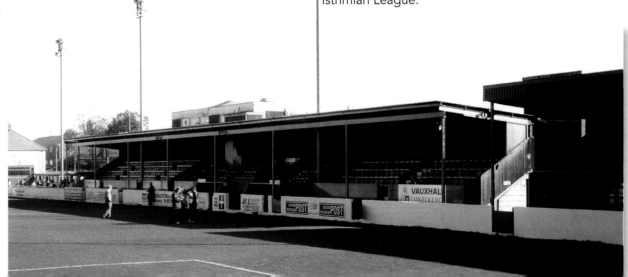

This picture: North Stand, 1993.

*Opposite: Victoria Road's
Pondfield End, 1993.*

Although the ground continued to be regularly maintained, not a great deal of the infrastructure changed until the arrival of Redbridge Forest in 1990 to ground share. The Redbridge Forest club came into being as a result of a merger between the Leytonstone/Ilford and Walthamstow Avenue teams in 1979. The incoming club paid for a new stand to be erected in the corner of the ground to increase the seating capacity and they replaced the grass banking with concrete terracing.

These improvements brought the ground up to the standard required by the Football Conference. Dagenham were in financial difficulty and in July 1992 merged with Redbridge Forest. Ground improvements continued right up to the present day. In 1995, they replaced the crumbling pitch perimeter wall with a new brick-built one and in 1997 the toilet block at the Victoria Road end of the ground was rebuilt.

The year 2001 saw significant enhancements to Victoria Road. The wooden south stand was now starting to look its age and the club decided it was time to demolish it and build a new purpose-built one. The new 800 all-seater, which brought the club's overall seating capacity to over 1,000, was used for the first time for the Essex Senior Cup final against Canvey Island on 4 August 2001, just 12 weeks after the old stand saw its last game. The teams' dugouts were situated at the front of it, and the stand comprised six rows of seating having a small executive area at the back. The stand ran for three quarters of the length of the pitch.

At the Pondfield Road end of this side, another separate stand existed. This stand, which is the Family Stand, was a small covered, seated stand. It was smaller in height than the Main Stand with some supporting pillars and contained around 200 seats. The club continued to improve the facilities and the summer of 2001 saw the construction of new turnstile blocks and the replacement of the eight floodlights, which used to sit on the sides of the ground, with four corner ones.

In October 2001 Bass Brewers PLC agreed a record-breaking £150,000 sponsorship of the new Main Stand, now named the Carling Stand. This provided the funds for improvements to continue, and a number of crush barriers were installed in 2002, which helped ease the flow of spectators around the ground, along with a new walkway behind the covered terrace. Also constructed was a new turnstile block at the Bury Road End of the ground. These improvements enabled the ground to meet Football League criteria. This was timely as John Still's team rose in prominence, eventually overcoming all in the Conference to at last win promotion to the Football League at the end of the 2006–07 season.

The most notable improvement following election saw the Traditional Builders Stand replace the open terracing at the western end of the ground (the Pondfield End), a sizeable affair that opened in December 2009. The all-seater stand, with windshields to either side, accommodated around 1,200 supporters and was also now the home of the dressing rooms used on matchdays.

That season heralded Dagenham's promotion to League One in 2010. Sadly they lasted only one season at the higher level. The floodlights were replaced in the summer of 2012 which brought the Chigwell Construction Stadium fully up to the new Football League regulations with regards to floodlighting.

The North Stand has remained much as it was 50 years before, and is known affectionately as 'The Sieve' due to the roof's famed ability at one time to let in water. The uncovered home terrace, the Bury Road End (aka the Clock End), has seen little change and now has a small basic electric scoreboard situated above it. This area also contains the club shop and police control box.

After five years in League Two, the club slipped out of the league in 2016, but made the play-offs in the Vanarama National League in 2016–17, eyeing a possible swift return.

Darlington

Feethams

Address: Victoria Embankment, Darlington DL1 5JR

Highest attendance: 21,023 v Bolton Wanderers, 14 November 1960

First league match: Darlington 2-0 v Halifax Town, 27 August 1921

Final league match: Darlington 2-2 v Leyton Orient, 3 May 2003

International matches: England amateur (1907)

Other usages: County Cricket

Ground layout: North Stand (Tin Shed), South Stand (Polam Lane End), East Stand, West Stand

Status: Demolished

Current stadium: Blackwell Meadows

Right: The North Stand in the 1960s.

Opposite: The new East Stand, 2003.

Darlington spent 120 years at Feethams, alongside the town's cricket club who owned the ground. The actual word Feethams means 'near the water', and the ground was built right next to the river Skerne and on an area called Feethams House.

The two sports grounds stood side by side, with fans having to walk through Darlington's 'twin towers' built in 1913, and around the cricket field, to get to the football action. The stadium was a throwback to football's early days, fitting for a team that had been residents of England's fourth tier for two decades. The club originally played in regionally organised leagues, and were one of the founding members of the Northern League in 1889. They were first admitted to the Football League when the Third Division North was formed in 1921.

There were four sections to the ground: the West Stand, the all-seated East Stand, Polam Lane (South) End and the 'Tin Shed' home terrace (the Cricket Ground End). The most modern stand, the East Stand, was rebuilt in 1997 and was the major cause of the club's financial difficulties.

The East Stand was the most impressive, costing £3 million with 'DARLINGTON' adorning the black and white seats. Its predecessor had been erected in 1919, taking five years to build owing to the club's financial situation, and ran along only two-thirds of the pitch with open terracing either side. It also contained offices and changing rooms underneath. But the construction of the new East Stand almost crippled Darlington financially.

The North Stand, or 'Tin Shed' as it was known, accommodated the more vocal home fans and backed on to the cricket ground; the simple cantilevered cover was put over the shallow Cricket Field End terrace in 1960. At the same time, floodlights arrived, thought to have come from Hull City. Both of these developments were made possible by the supporters' club who raised £20,000. The Polam Lane End terrace opposite, built in 1905, was open to the elements.

The West Stand had a more eventful history. Originally built at the turn of the 20th century, it was destroyed by fire on the night of Darlington's first floodlit match, a 5–2 triumph over Millwall. An

50

electrical fault was blamed, and an exact replica was constructed the following year, this time built almost entirely from wood.

After a mediocre existence of more than four decades after the Second World War, the club's incoming chairman George Reynolds eventually spent £18 million moving the Quakers to the 25,500 all-seater Reynolds Arena in 2003, though he left the club under a cloud shortly after it opened, serving time in prison for tax evasion, and administration followed for the club. The decadent Arena, the whitest of white elephants, was described as a 'hollow shell of a place next to a motorway'. The new stadium had a record attendance of 11,600, set during a Division Three game against Kidderminster Harriers in 2003, and an average of around 4,000. The club went into administration six months after moving to the Arena.

Feethams remained without a tenant for three years, but the football ground was eventually demolished in 2006 shortly after an arson attack on the West Stand. The East Stand was dismantled and sold on to Farnborough FC, the floodlights were sold to Workington AFC, while the cricket ground remained in use.

In 2009, overcoming a 1903 Deed of Foundation retaining Feethams as a sports facility, the board sold the football field to developers, who then subsequently sold the land in 2013. In an unpopular sale, local pressure groups tried in vain to get the football club back to Feethams and to protect the surrounding green spaces. But in 2014, a national building company lodged a planning application to construct over 80 homes on the site, and construction was underway in 2015, due for completion in 2016.

In the meantime, the poor road access at the renamed Darlington Arena saw council planners restrict the capacity of the stadium to just 10,000 on match days. In February 2009 Darlington again went into administration, triggering an automatic 10-point deduction, without which they would have again reached the play-offs. A deal was brokered to come

out of administration allowing Darlington to compete in the 2009–10 season, but with resources cut to the bone, they finished bottom and dropped out of the Football League in 2010.

A little more than two months later, the newest owner placed the club into administration for a third time in less than a decade. Two days later, the club was spared from liquidation after a last-minute injection of funding by supporters' groups, enough for Darlington to complete the season, but relegation was confirmed with three matches remaining.

After the club was taken over with the intention of moving into community ownership, without entering into a CVA, Darlington were relegated four divisions to the Northern League Division One on the recommendation of the Football Association. On 21 June 2012 the Football Association rejected an appeal, confirming that the club was to be treated as a 'new club' entered into the Northern League, and would

no longer be able to play under the name Darlington FC. The new owners opted to rename the new club Darlington 1883 – the year the club was founded.

In 2012, Darlington left the Arena ground and moved temporarily to nearby Bishop Auckland instead, sharing their Heritage Park ground. On 18 March 2016, it was confirmed that Darlington would be returning to the town to Blackwell Meadows during the 2016–17 season (ground-sharing with Darlington RFC), with expansion plans in place which would expand Blackwell Meadows to hold 3,000 fans, which are the regulations in order to be promoted to the Vanarama National League North. Darlington 1883 have won three promotions in the last four years, and sit in a promising position in the Vanarama National League North. There is now a fighting chance that Darlington could soon return to the Football League.

Reynolds Arena/Darlington Arena - see page 156.

The North Terrace, 1992.

Feethams Stadium, 1989.

The West Stand.

Old East Stand, 1993.

Derby County

Baseball Ground

Address: Shaftesbury Crescent, Derby, Derbyshire DE23 8GU

Highest attendance: 41,826 v Tottenham Hotspur, 20 September 1969

First league match: Derby County 0–1 v Sunderland, 19 March 1892

Final league match: Derby County 1–3 v Arsenal, 11 May 1997

International matches: England (1911)

Other usages: Baseball

Ground layout: Main Stand, Popular Side/ East Stand (Ley Stand), Osmaston End, Normanton End

Status: Demolished

Current stadium: Pride Park

Former league champions and FA Cup winners Derby County called the Baseball Ground home for over a century. As its name suggests, the stadium was used to play a sport more commonly associated with America. The football club originally played on a pitch that was part of the Derbyshire Cricket Club which at that time was in the middle of a racecourse.

Derby's first league match at the ground was in 1892, a 1–0 defeat to Sunderland, after there was a fixture clash at the racecourse which at the time saw horses take priority. The Rams moved in permanently in 1895, sharing with Derby County Baseball Club, but it wasn't for long, as their bat-and-ball-playing cohabitants folded three years later.

The stadium was originally called Ley's Baseball Ground and was part of a complex of sports grounds (Ley's Recreation Ground) built and owned by businessman Sir Francis Ley for workers at his foundry. After Derby moved in, Ley invested £7,000 to raise the capacity from 4,000 to 20,000. The ground became the property of the club in 1924 when it was purchased from Ley's heirs for £10,000. It was famous for having a difficult pitch, in part a consequence of the playing area being below street level and creating drainage problems.

Soon after purchasing the ground, Derby were promoted to the First Division in 1926 and seized the opportunity to build a new Main Stand designed by Archibald Leitch. Work began immediately on this stand, known as B Pavilion, with a frontage

Right: The Osmaston End, 1989.

on Shaftesbury Crescent. The dressing rooms and offices were moved under it so that, for the first time at the Baseball Ground, players emerged from the side rather than an end.

After the stand had been completed, attention was then turned to the opposite side (Popular Side). The terracing was deepened towards the front, with gangways going across, and a roof was built later, with a higher step in the centre. The roof offered advertising space.

Derby's crowds kept growing though and in 1933 a new double-decker stand was built at the Osmaston End, affectionately known as the 'Ossie End', although it did not fill the entire width. The north-eastern section, known as Catcher's Corner from the baseball days, remained uncovered. There was a small hut and a platform, in front of which half-time scores were displayed.

Two years a later a very similar double-decker stand was built at the opposite end, the Normanton End, except that the latter slanted backwards from the pitch, a quirk from the days of baseball giving the ground a wedge shape. Therefore, in less than a decade the capacity had increased from around 20,000 to 38,000.

During the construction of the three stands, plans for a new multi-purpose stadium were already being proposed, but bomb damage to the Osmaston End in January 1941 during a German air-raid put paid to this. The stand remained out of commission as the Rams made their way towards the 1946 FA Cup final. Little changed after the war apart from the installation of floodlights, set low on the corners of the end stands in 1953.

However, under manager Brian Clough and a side captained to the Second Division championship by former Spurs warhorse Dave Mackay, a new East Stand (The Popular Side) was extensively redeveloped in 1969 and named in honour of Ley. Derby obtained enough land from their neighbours to make the construction feasible, but so cramped was the site

that access to the seats was possible only with walkways above the terracing. The redevelopment had increased capacity to just over 40,000, and the Baseball Ground was one of the few English stadiums with seating as well as standing areas on all sides. Three years later, the stadium witnessed Derby win the league twice in quick succession in 1972 and 1975 – the club's finest hours.

Entry into the European Cup in 1972 compelled the installation of new floodlights to match UEFA specifications. This development was a considerable relief to press photographers, who had struggled through the gloom of outmoded lights for years.

From the mid-1970s Derby's sporting successes and finances slowly deteriorated and so did their home. The hemmed-in stadium with access difficulties was slowly converted to become all-seater from terracing and had a reduced capacity of 18,300 following the Taylor Report.

The confines of the Baseball Ground made conversion difficult, as the ground was far from suited to becoming an all-seater, and led to many discomforts. After plans were mooted to move the club, which did not advance quickly, alternative plans were made in 1995 to rebuild three of the four stands leaving only the recent Ley Stand intact. Chairman Lionel Pickering had ambitious plans to boost Derby's current stadium capacity by rebuilding it as a 26,000-seat venue.

In the end though County, then back in the Premier League, opted instead for a move to the 33,000-capacity Pride Park Stadium on the outskirts of town in 1997. The relocation plan had only been unveiled some 18 months before the new stadium was opened.

The last league match to be played at the old ground was a top-flight fixture against Arsenal in May. The Baseball Ground remained in use for County's reserve games before it was finally demolished in 2003. The site was redeveloped to accommodate around 150 new homes, and in September 2010

a commemorative statue was unveiled there. The 4.5m-high metalwork statue features the silhouettes of three footballers dribbling and shooting. As a tribute, all the new roads were named in connection with the football club.

The new purpose-built Pride Park home costing £28 million would be for football only, where fans would be hoping it would be goals, not home runs, raining in. Derby County currently occupy a place in the Championship.

Above: The Baseball Ground, Derby. The Main Stand, August 1990.

Opposite top: The Normanton End, August 1991.

Opposite bottom: The East Stand/Co-op Stand, 1992.

Doncaster Rovers

Belle Vue

Below: The Rossington End, 1989.

Right: Town End Stand, 1971.

Doncaster Rovers moved into Belle Vue from their temporary Bennetthorpe Ground in 1922 whilst playing in the Midland League. The ground had an eventful history and witnessed Doncaster's rapid rise up the league at the turn of the century, though Rovers had moved out before their ascent to the Championship. The stadium literally went out with a bang in 2007, a year after its tenants had left, when gas filled the ground after a boiler was stolen; the resulting explosion sped up the demolition process.

The ground was opened by Charles E. Sutcliffe from the Football League on Saturday, 26 August 1922, when the Midland League opposition was Gainsborough Trinity. The initial capacity was 7,000 spectators, which was then extended year-on-year as the club's finances allowed. Rovers were promoted back to the Football League's Third Division North at the end of that season. A trace of Rovers' Bennetthorpe history could still be seen at Belle Vue as late as 1985, as five years after arriving in 1922 the club jacked up the old Main Stand and transported it on rollers from their old home and deposited it on the North Terrace (Town End) behind the goal, forming The Family Stand. Large amounts of ash were transported from nearby coal tips to create banking and a foundation for the pitch.

The ground was renowned for having one of the top-five biggest pitches in the country, at 110 yards long and 72 yards wide. In addition to the size of the pitch, it was considered to have one of the best playing surfaces due to the fertile soil.

In 1938 the capacity of Belle Vue was increased to 40,000 and it was in 1948 that the stadium recorded its highest attendance of 37,149, against Hull City.

The ground consisted of the Main Stand, which had a good-sized strip of terracing running the full length of the pitch, and situated behind that, an elevated section of wooden seating. Over both of these areas a large roof gave shelter to both the seats and the terrace. Behind both goals were two similar looking areas of terracing, one covered originally then both open, neither stretching that far back; one was the Town End Terrace, and the other the Rossington End.

Completing the picture, opposite the Main Stand, was the Popular Terrace. As with the two ends, the terracing didn't stretch that far back but, unlike the end stands, it was covered by a roof that ran for the length of the pitch.

In the later years of the 20th century, as the club's fortunes began to decline and finances became tighter, the capacity of Belle Vue was cut dramatically, falling as low as 4,859 in May 1987 when mining subsidence was found underground beneath the Popular Stand terrace. The Town End family stand was demolished in 1985 after the fire at Bradford, when wooden stands were finally deemed unsafe.

Despite this precaution, Belle Vue's Main Stand was set ablaze a decade later following an evening match against Fulham. It caused extensive damage. The chairman at the time, Ken Richardson, was later arrested and charged with conspiracy to commit arson; a court later found he had hired a former SAS soldier to douse it in petrol. Richardson withdrew his financial backing and as a result the club was subject to an administration order. The fire and the chairman's act were said to have been major factors in Doncaster dropping out of the Football League in 1998. The stand was repaired and rebuilt where necessary.

During this period until the ground closure, Belle Vue was also the home of the newly re-formed rugby league side Doncaster Dragons.

After five seasons in the Conference League, the club returned to the Football League after winning the 2003 Conference play-off final. In the summer of 2003 work began to repair the Town End terrace, to replace the old seating in the Main Stand and to extend the Rossington End terrace.

In 2003–04, the first season back in the Football League, Rovers achieved promotion to the third tier as champions. In the summer of 2004, the Popular Stand terrace was also extended and executive boxes were built at the Town End of the stadium. New club offices, a new supporters' bar and the application of tarmac to the car park completed a much needed facelift. In a move that dismayed some Belle Vue fans the ground was renamed Earth Stadium as part of a sponsorship deal with Rotherham-based finance company Earth Finance. The capacity reached the region of 11,500.

However, a new stadium had long been mooted for Doncaster Rovers and this finally started to become a reality when planning permission was granted. Construction began on 17 October 2005 of a 15,000 all-seater community stadium complex. The new ground was named the Keepmoat Stadium.

The last ever game at Belle Vue was on 23 December 2006. The stadium was left to decay but a year after vacation another flame-related incident occurred when, as previously mentioned, the Main Stand, which had survived the arson attempt a dozen years earlier, exploded after the aforementioned boiler theft.

Following the explosion, demolition of the stadium was rapidly accelerated and very little remained of the ground. Areas of terrace were still identifiable and large sections of the pitch remained, but The Main Stand and Popular Side were reduced to rubble, and floodlights, executive boxes, turnstiles, snack bars and offices were either removed or destroyed, along with the ground's club house, The Rover's Return. The site was patrolled by security following the explosion and was fenced off whilst demolition work was undertaken. After demolition, the security fences remained in place to prevent access to the site.

After six years of stagnation and with the site becoming an eyesore, a nationally-profiled property developer purchased Belle Vue from the council in 2013 for housing.

The club's move to the Keepmoat Stadium in 2006 didn't stall their momentum as they secured another promotion in 2008 back to the Championship, after an absence of 50 years, just five years after returning to the Football League. However, since that time the club has experienced a rather yo-yo existence, with several relegations and promotions. However, they ended the 2016–17 season on a high, winning automatic promotion back to League One.

The Main Stand, 1971.

Gateshead

Redheugh Park

Right: Redheugh Park before it closed in 1960.

*Opposite: A football pitch remains on the site of
Redheugh Park.*

In a part of the country where the supporters are famed for their passion for the game, there was once another venue for fans in the north east to view league football – Redheugh Park, home of Gateshead AFC.

Sites at Low Fell and Sheriff Hill were considered, but were deemed too far out of town. The chosen location was in the Teams area of Gateshead, a worked-out clay pit (known as Johnson's Clay Hole) edged by Ropery Road and Derwentwater Road. The holes, tunnels and craters on the site were filled by lorries full of the town's refuse.

Born from the ashes of cash-strapped league side South Shields FC, who relocated from Horsley Hill in search of greater support, Gateshead kicked off in the Third Division North at Redheugh in 1930. The oval-shaped stadium owned by the council with terracing throughout was built specifically for their arrival. Cover was provided on three sides.

The Main Stand was a two-thirds-pitch-length seated stand (purchased from a greyhound stadium in Carlisle) with covered standing extensions added on either side. Opposite the Main Stand was a large covered terrace that ran the full length of the ground. The North End of the ground had a small covered terrace, whilst the opposite Ropery Road (South) End was a small uncovered terrace, which was upgraded in 1937 and included a large Totalisator scoreboard introduced for greyhound racing.

Gateshead were another club to allow greyhound

racing to occupy their home as a means of boosting revenue to assist in maintaining the stadium; however this meant that the stadium capacity was reduced as the new elliptical shape affected pitch and terrace size. Despite this introduction, finances continued to be a major worry.

The club's finest hour saw them reach the quarter-finals of the FA Cup in 1953 when they lost narrowly to eventual finalists Bolton Wanderers and the mighty Nat Lofthouse at Redheugh Park.

With crowds steadily dwindling and success on the pitch not forthcoming, Gateshead finished 22nd in the Fourth Division in 1960 and were forced to apply for re-election along with Southport, Hartlepool and Oldham. Despite their good record and confidence, they were surprisingly not successful and were voted out of the Football League, being replaced by Peterborough United. Gateshead then failed in an application to join the Scottish League.

With the loss of Football League status and the football club's subsequent continual slide down the leagues, a further heavy blow was dealt with the cessation of greyhound racing at the stadium in 1966. This put both Redheugh Park and Gateshead AFC in serious financial difficulty. Other sources of income were investigated, and in 1967 the club made a vain attempt to fill the void that greyhound racing had left by staging speedway racing at the stadium.

Five years later the stadium was in a derelict condition and vandalised, with crumbling terraces and dilapidated stands, and the pitch was weed infested. This, coupled with a fire, saw Gateshead AFC relocate to the Gateshead Youth Stadium (now the International Athletics Stadium), and the stadium stands were demolished in 1972. The club's tenure at the new venue was to be very short lived, however, and the club went into liquidation in 1973.

From this carnage, a re-formed South Shields FC, then playing in the Northern Premier League, relocated to the Youth Stadium in 1974 and became Gateshead United FC, although this too was short lived and the club went out of business just three years later. A new Gateshead FC was formed to take their place, and it is this incarnation that has endured to this day.

The last four decades have seen the club bounce around a host of various Northern non-league divisions, but they eventually reached the Conference. In 2013–14, Gateshead agonisingly missed out on a return to the Football League when they lost narrowly to Cambridge United in the Conference play-off final at Wembley.

The club still sits more than comfortably in the Vanarama National League, and one good season may yet see the famous name of Gateshead return to the Football League after an absence of more than half a century.

The site of Redheugh Park was completely flattened for the 1990 Gateshead Garden Festival, but a football pitch still exists on the site today and appropriately a five-a-side soccer centre is resident nearby.

Halifax Town   The Shay

Address: The Shay Ground, Halifax, West Yorkshire HX1 2YS

Highest attendance: 36,885 v Tottenham Hotspur (FA Cup), 14 February 1953

First league match: Halifax Town 5-0 v Darlington, 3 September 1921

Final league match: Halifax Town 2-4 v Rushden & Diamonds FC, 20 April 2002

Other usages: Speedway, Rugby League

Ground-sharing: Halifax Rugby League Club

Ground layout: North Stand, South Stand, East Stand, Skircoat Stand (West Stand)

Status: Extant

Current stadium: The Shay (The MBi Shay Stadium)

Right: Skircoat Road Stand, 1971.

Opposite top: The Shay, 1989.

Opposite bottom: The East Stand in the 1970s, with speedway still in evidence.

The name Shay was derived from the old English word 'shaw', which means a small wood, and the ground spent most of its Football League existence in a rather dilapidated state; work on renovating the stadium was never top of the list for a club whose primary objective was to retain Football League status. It was during its second stint as a league venue that work began to pick up and continued even after its tenant, Halifax Town AFC, went out of business in 2008.

Halifax Town, formed in 1911, had earlier played at Sandhall Lane and then Exley, a totally unsuitable venue. Initially they played in the Yorkshire Combination and the Midland League. The stadium, set into the side of a hill on the south side of Halifax about a quarter of a mile from the town centre, was built, like many, on a former council rubbish tip and

was completed in time for Halifax's debut season in the League, 1921-22, the founding season of the newly-formed Third Division North. It witnessed a stunning opening match, the hosts beating Darlington 5–0. Its Main Stand was purchased from Manchester City, still at their old stadium of Hyde Road, while behind the goal was open terracing.

In 1949 the Shay introduced speedway into its repertoire, with the pitch size being reduced; yet the track proved bothersome for football as even the fans at the front of the stands were still 30ft away from the pitch, hindering the stadium's acoustics. It is said that one Halifax manager wanted to play crowd noise from Wembley over the Tannoy to improve the atmosphere! The initial speedway venture was unsuccessful, terminating after just three years. Ten years later, Middlesbrough speedway promoter Reg

to supermarkets and property developers during the 1980s and the local council appeared none too helpful in accepting proposals. In 1986 the club was close to collapse and the council's view thankfully changed. The council took over the Shay in 1987, it becoming part of Calderdale Leisure Services (CLS), and in July 1988 new plans were announced for the ground. A new stand was purchased from Scunthorpe United, and other major ground improvements were being made. Despite some certainty for the ground, on the pitch Halifax Town were relegated from the Football League in 1993.

Ultimately it was the fans, the Football Trust, who provided funds for redevelopment, and the arrival of Halifax's Rugby League Club that allowed the ground to be finally brought up to date. Upon Halifax's return to the Football League after a five-year absence in 1998, the North Stand was built, and the new all-seater South Stand, complete with cantilever roof, was built a year later behind the goal. The old Family Stand was demolished in 2000 and work on a new covered, single-tiered seated Main Stand holding 3,500 on the East side began.

Sadly on the pitch, it was a sojourn for Halifax Town, and they lost Football League status again in 2002. Unfortunately for the club and stadium, work stalled on the East Stand following relegation and it remained unfinished. Halifax Town was placed into

administration in 2007 and were wound up in 2008, after debts of over £2 million proved insurmountable.

A newly-formed FC Halifax Town replaced them and went on to play at the ground in the Northern Premier League Division One (North) in 2008–09. FC Halifax Town enjoyed considerable success after 2010 rising three divisions to sit just outside the Football League once again. The East Stand finally opened in March 2010, bringing the venue back to the heart of Calderdale's sporting and community life.

The old Skircoat Stand has been turned into an all-seated affair, and although no plans for future redevelopment have been officially announced, there has been talk of a new west stand to replace it. The potential plan is to build a two-tier stand with shops that back on to Skircoat Road.

FC Halifax Town were unfortunately relegated again at the end of the 2015–16 season, to the National League North, and, at the time, disputes with the council could have seen the rugby club leaving the Shay. Fortunately, events took a better turn at the end of the 2016–17 season and FC Halifax were promoted straight back to the National League via the play-offs.

Fearman saw the Shay for the first time and made a formal application to Halifax Town for use of the ground to revive the sport.

At the beginning of 1965, work began on re-constructing the ground and speedway returned. Second time around it proved successful, and remained at the Shay for the next 20 years. By the 1970s, people valued the speedway more highly than football for family entertainment, with the Dukes producing such great riders as Eric Boocock and the late great Kenny Carter.

Attendances were regularly higher than those of the football club and the Shay often hosted speedway internationals. In 1986, after disputes over money with the struggling football club, speedway waved goodbye to the Shay for the last time moving to neighbouring Bradford as the Bradford Dukes.

The stadium had become a hindrance for the club; several former chairmen attempted to sell it

Hereford United

Edgar Street

Address: Athletic Ground, Edgar Street, Hereford, Herefordshire HR4 9JU

Highest attendance: 18,114 v Sheffield Wednesday, 4 January 1958 (FA Cup)

First league match: Hereford United 3-0 v Reading, 19 August 1972

Final league match: Hereford United 3-2 v Torquay United, 5 May 2012

Other usages: Pop festival (1971)

Ground layout: The Cargill Stand, Merton Meadow Stand (Merton Stand), Merton Meadow Terrace (Meadow End), Blackfriars End

Status: Extant

Current stadium: Edgar Street

Right: Len Weston Stand, 1977.

Opposite top: Merton Stand, 1994.

Opposite bottom: Meadow End, 1997.

Such was the popularity of football in the town during the early 1900s that four leading amateur teams emerged: Hereford City FC, Hereford Thistle FC, St Martins and RAOC (Rotherwas). They all used Edgar Street as did the athletics club who owned the ground. However, due to its location and a lack of focused interest it was comparatively late that a senior football team was formed – and this was Hereford United, founded in 1924.

The club was an amalgamation of two of those local clubs, St Martins and RAOC, and was the first semi-professional football side in the county. Edgar Street became their home, initially sharing with City whilst the athletics activity ceased. Hereford paid their landlord the princely sum of £82 and 2 shillings in rent (£82.10p) that first season.

They quickly joined the Birmingham Combination. The new team played their first match, against Atherstone Town, on 20 August 1924. The following year saw the construction of a diminutive barrel-roofed stand, nicknamed 'Noah's Ark', on the Edgar Street side of the ground, plus a tin-roofed terrace opposite, known as the Cowshed.

United struggled financially during their early seasons and had to launch several public appeals to stay afloat. Their landlords helped out by reducing their rent until by the 1929–30 season they were only paying £14 7s 0d. (£14.35p) per year. However, in June 1931, the city council bought the ground for £3,000 from the Hereford Athletic Ground Company and rented it back to United at a much higher rent of £126 per season, reducing each season to £93 at the end of the 1937–38 season, just before war broke out.

After the war, the council set the rent at just over £100. From 1966 onwards the council set a revised and realistic rate each year. Once the athletics tracks

had been turfed over, Hereford had one of the widest pitches in the league. The pitch also had a distinctive and formidable downhill slope.

The early 1950s were exciting times for Hereford United after joining the Southern League. They won the Southern League Cup during the 1951–52 season, and in March 1952 the council granted United a 14-year lease at a peppercorn rate of £1 per season. The following season, floodlit football arrived at Edgar Street, long before many league clubs.

The lights were donated by local firm Painter Brothers, who specialised in constructing steel towers; their work included the Skylon which was built for the Festival of Britain in 1951. The floodlights were switched on for a Birmingham League fixture with Walsall Reserves in March 1953.

Hereford were always a top-class non-league side, causing many cup upsets in the 1950s putting out league sides including a 6-1 win at Queens Park Rangers in 1957–58, the widest margin win by a non-league side over a league one. As they progressed as a club, they sold land on the Edgar Street side in 1968 to make way for a road widening scheme. The 'Noah's Ark' stand set sail to nearby Risbury, being used as a barn on farmland, and a new cantilever stand with 1,200 seats was built as the Merton Meadow Stand (Merton Stand). This replaced the old Cowshed terraces. This was a raised, covered single-tier, all-seated stand. It was used as a family stand and had the team dugouts located in front. The club offices, hospitality, boardroom and changing rooms were underneath the stand.

In 1972 the Bulls caused one of the biggest FA Cup shocks in history in a third-round replay at Edgar Street. After taking a late lead through Malcolm Macdonald, First Division Newcastle United looked destined to go through, but with only eight minutes left, Ronnie Radford unleashed a cracking shot from 35 yards to put the game into extra time, when substitute Ricky George scored the winner. In the fourth round the Bulls were drawn against First

Division West Ham and were unluckily defeated in a replay.

That same season, and on the back of those cup exploits, the club won election to the Football League at the expense of Barrow. When the club progressed into the Football League the Merton Stand was extended to cover the entire length of the pitch.

The old wooden grandstand was replaced in 1974 with The Len Weston Stand, which was named after the former benefactor and club president. At this time, Edgar Street was the only ground outside the First Division to have two cantilever stands. The stand ran pitch length, and consisted of a terrace below an upper tier of seats which gave partial shelter to those standing underneath. The terrace had concrete supporting pillars which meant a restricted view in some areas. There was also a section put by for away supporters at the south side. The stand was later re-named the Cargill Stand. The stand had a 2,000 capacity.

The home end, named The Meadow End or the Merton Meadow Terrace, was a classic looking, partly-covered (to the rear) stand. This stand was semi-circular in shape, reflecting the previous athletics track going out around the back of the goal, and had a number of supporting pillars.

Opposite was the Blackfriars End, another partly-covered terrace, with a similar shape.

With two promotions in four years, United reached the giddy heights of the old Second Division, being sixth on one occasion. However in that first season, 1976–77, they ultimately finished bottom, and decline began as the club plunged back down to the Fourth Division in successive seasons. Worse was to come as they had to apply for re-election three times between 1980 and 1983.

The club spent 19 years in the bottom division, suffering financial problems in the early 1980s which resurfaced in the mid-1990s. Despite reaching the play-offs in 1995–96, but with the financial problems worsening, the club lost key players for the following season. After a terrible run of form, Hereford were ultimately relegated from the Football League after a final-day relegation-decider at Edgar Street with Brighton, thus ending a 25-year stay.

After nine years as a non-league club, Hereford returned to the top level in 2006 after a dramatic 3–2 victory over Halifax Town in the Conference play-off final. In their second season back in the Football League, Hereford won promotion to League One. Their revival was short lived and in 2012 they were again relegated to the Conference.

The ground was now aged and began to fall into disrepair. The Blackfriars End had already had its capacity reduced and had been closed in 2009–10 after failing a health and safety inspection. In June 2014, beset by debts, Hereford were expelled from the Conference after their new owners declined to put up a £350,000 bond. They were accepted into the seventh-tier Southern Premier League, but still faced a winding-up order.

On 19 December 2014, Hereford United were formally wound up and its record expunged from the Southern League. As was widely expected, a phoenix club was set up by the Hereford United Supporters Trust with support from local businesses and the local authority who granted them the lease on Edgar Street in March 2015. Hereford FC were admitted to the Midland Football League, the ninth tier in the English pyramid, for the 2015–16 season. Support was very encouraging and promotion achieved to the Southern League First Division (South and West). Season 2016–17 saw a second successive promotion to the Southern Premier Division as runaway champions, the team losing just once all season and scoring more than 100 league goals.

The long-term aim for the club is to progress back to the Football League as quickly as possible, but in a sustainable manner.

Edgar Street's Merton Stand, 1969.

Huddersfield Town   Leeds Road

Address: Old Fieldhouse Lane, Huddersfield, West Yorkshire HD1 1AG

Highest attendance: 67,037 v Arsenal (FA Cup), 27 February 1932

First league match: Huddersfield Town 0–1 v Burnley, 10 September 1910

Final league match: Huddersfield Town 2–1 v Blackpool, 30 April 1994

International matches: England (1946)

Other usages: Rugby League (1992–1994)

Ground layout: Main Stand, East Stand/Popular Terrace, Leeds Road End, Dalton Bank End

Status: Demolished

Current stadium: Galpharm Stadium (The John Smith's Stadium)

Right: Dalton Bank End, 1981, showing the replacement manual scoreboard.

Leeds Road was once home to the most feared team in England. When Huddersfield Town won their third league championship in a row less than 20 years after being formed, their home ground was today's equivalent to Old Trafford. Acquired in 1908, it was little more than a field with an old tramcar doubling up as a changing room and a ticket office, but upon gaining entry to the Football League in 1910, Huddersfield began work on Leitch-inspired designs for a new stadium.

Leitch's plans involved the construction of a 4,000-seater covered Main Stand with a terraced paddock at one side of the pitch. A gable was also to be added to the pitched roof, similar to his earlier designs for Fulham, Chelsea and Tottenham. The Leeds Road End was to have a partly covered terrace (to the rear), and two open banks of terracing were to be provided for the other sides of the ground. The total capacity was to be around 34,000. The club were given admittance to the Football League and work began on the ground in June 1910, in line with Leitch's plans.

With the pitch rotated 90 degrees and a newly-covered West Stand, Leeds Road opened fully in 1911. The capacity was seldom filled however, owing to the town's preference for rugby league. Rapid spending coupled with disappointing gate returns saw Huddersfield slip into administration the following year, their future at Leeds Road seemingly in doubt, and a potential move to Elland Road on the cards. The crisis was averted, however, and success on the pitch brought frequent attendance records. By the 1920s, Leeds Road was the home of the three-times English champions with crowds regularly topping 30,000.

Despite these league successes, ground improvements were extremely modest. During 1929 the Leeds Road End was given a new barrel-shaped roof which covered the whole of the terrace. The

and barriers. A single post-war international match took place at the ground on a Wednesday afternoon in 1946, when England defeated Netherlands 8–2 in a friendly.

In 1950, the roof and upper tier of the Main Stand were destroyed after the north-west corner of the ground caught fire. However, the ground was empty save for a few hastily evacuated employees. This was replaced by a similar looking structure, although unfortunately without the gable.

The last major construction at Leeds Road occurred during a brief return to the First Division in 1955, when a vast cover was built over the Popular Side. Costing £24,000, this covered 20,000 fans.

At the same time, at the Dalton Bank End, the country's first-ever electric scoreboard to be installed at a football ground arrived. Dutch Company Phillips had given it to the club as a gift. Philips had a factory in Darwen and their PSV Eindhoven team had close ties with Huddersfield Town. Regrettably, the gift was vandalised in 1970 and replaced by a traditional manual board.

Floodlights were erected in 1961, and were nicknamed the 'Denis Law Lights'. It was part of the proceeds of his £55,000 transfer fee to Manchester City that funded their installation. They were first used in an FA Cup third-round replay on Wednesday 11 January 1961 when 46,155 turned up to see the Terriers beat Wolves.

The floodlighting system cost £23,000 to install and was ready just a few hours before the start of the match. In February the following year two of the floodlights blew down in a gale, one embedding itself in the pitch.

The creation of seating in the West Stand paddock in 1970 and the inclusion of a television gantry gave Leeds Road the appearance it would keep until it was vacated 24 years later. The capacity fell to 31,000 following the Safety of Sports Grounds Act in 1984. Town, who had inhabited the Fourth Division during the period, were lucky to get half the capacity figure

wooden roof led to the end being nicknamed the Cowshed by the supporters, a name which stuck until the ground was closed in 1994. The other terraces were also further expanded.

The East Terrace (also known as the Popular Terrace) was extended so that it was 126 steps high. The other terrace, the Dalton Bank End, was also extended but on a smaller scale and was to remain uncovered.

In 1931 the directors purchased a 1,300-seat stand from Fleetwood for just £170. Huddersfield's set of second-hand rows was to be re-erected at the top of the Dalton Bank terrace, but fortunately

for those who enjoyed free views of the game from Dalton Bank itself behind the ground, the foundations proved to be unsuitable. Instead, the stand was made into an L-shaped enclosure for schoolboys and tucked into a corner between the new barrel roof and the West Stand.

Still, these improvements boosted the ground's capacity, and in 1932 over 67,000 fans crammed in to watch an FA Cup tie against Arsenal. It may have been more, as a number of fans broke down gates on the Popular Side and got into the ground for nothing. Five years later, a barrier collapsed during an FA Cup semi-final match, leading to an upgrade of the terraces and as the stadium fell away, the Cowshed was deemed unsafe in 1989 and would not re-open for two years.

A foretaste of the new ground-sharing era was provided when Huddersfield RLFC (Huddersfield Giants) played their first-ever rugby league game at Leeds Road in 1992, having left the now crumbling Fartown after 114 years.

In 1994 Huddersfield left Leeds Road for the modern all-seater Galpharm Stadium (then known as the Alfred McAlpine Stadium). Since then, the company Heineken have bought the sponsorship rights to the stadium and in August 2012 the stadium was renamed The John Smith's Stadium in a five-year arrangement.

A retail park now stands on the site of Leeds Road, with a plaque marking the location of the old centre circle. Nothing else at all remains to remind people of the 60,000 fans who once flocked there.

The Terriers have seen much better times of late, and after attaining a Championship play-off spot at the end of the 2016–17 season were promoted back into the top flight after a period of 45 years by winning the Championship play-off final.

Opposite: Huddersfield's Dalton Bank End, 1980s.

Below: Leeds Road End, 1992.

Hull City

Boothferry Park

Address: Boothferry Road, Kingston-upon-Hull HU4 6EU

Highest attendance: 55,019 v Manchester United, (FA Cup), 26 February 1949

First league match: Hull City 0-0 v Lincoln City, 31 August 1946

Final league match: Hull City 0-1 v Darlington, 14 December 2002

International matches: England U-23 (1970), Northern Ireland (1972)

Other usages: Rugby League internationals

Ground layout: North Stand, South Stand/Bunker's Hill Stand, East Stand/Kempton Stand, West Stand

Status: Demolished

Current stadium: KCOM Stadium

Right: East Stand, 1975.

Opposite: North Stand, July 1997.

Hull City finally moved into Boothferry Park in 1946, nearly two decades after plans were initially drawn up in 1929. Several factors including financial difficulties, the outbreak of the Second World War and post-war austerity hampered the move, but, upon settling, City made up for lost time; Boothferry's 20,000 capacity when opened had been almost trebled to 55,000 when it witnessed its record crowd against Manchester United three years later. The club had joined the Football League in 1905–06 and previously occupied a number of sites including the Boulevard and Anlaby Road Cricket Ground.

Initial work did not commence until 1932, when the terracing was started and the pitch laid out. Then in 1939 the plans were temporarily thrown into doubt because of a proposal to build a multi-purpose sports stadium on the site.

The ground was finally opened in August 1946, but only had planning permission for one stand along the west side with an upper cost limit of £17,000. The ground was still not fully completed and it became a race against time to make the stadium ready for its opening Third Division North match against visiting Lincoln City. The terracing embankments were subsequently raised and by February 1949 the stadium accommodated its record crowd, the team winning promotion at the end of the season.

The West Stand was referred to on the original plans for Boothferry Park as the 'Best Stand' and that

name stuck in the minds of many Hull City fans, as it housed the changing rooms, directors' area, press area, etc. Although a fairly simple design, being box-like in appearance, it served its purpose. The stand had windshields on either side, and a small television gantry was later incorporated into its roof.

A partial cover on the North Stand behind the goal was also in place for the ground's opening, with this goal-side cover being completed in 1950.

The following year the East Stand was erected, giving Boothferry three sides of cover. This was supposed to be a temporary structure but it was never replaced, and stood throughout the years of the ground. The popular east terrace became known as the Kempton Stand after the Kempton Road that ran behind it. The stand was a basic cover supported by pillars. It didn't run the full length of the stand, but to around each penalty area, with open terracing each side.

That same year saw the ground's very own railway station situated behind that East Stand open for business; Boothferry Halt was used for the first time for the visit of Everton. Six trains ran the football service between Paragon Station, Hull's central railway station, and Boothferry Park. Spectators could enter the ground via turnstiles on the station platform.

With the three stands completed, the ground was now ready for floodlight installation. Two gantries housing 96 lamps were built, one on the west and one opposite on the east. Although this lighting system was the envy of many clubs, advances in stadium lighting came rapidly, and the system soon needed replacing. A six-pylon system costing £50,000 replaced the old gantries in 1963. City were the only league side to possess six pylons.

The new lights were used for the first time in 1964, using four of the six available, for an evening match against Barnsley, a 7–0 win for the Tigers.

In 1965 a new state-of-the-art South Stand was built over the Bunker's Hill Terrace. The new two-tiered structure included a propped cantilever roof,

2,500 seats in the upper tier and terracing for 4,000 more in the lower tier. This stand, constructed with a gymnasium, made Boothferry Park the envy of most First Division clubs despite Hull City competing in the lower echelons of the league.

England U-23s played their Swedish counterparts at the ground in 1970, and on 16 February 1972 Boothferry Park hosted a full international match between Northern Ireland and Spain. The result was a 1–1 draw. Boothferry Park was also the scene of a rugby league international match when it hosted the first Ashes series test of the 1982 Kangaroo tour between Great Britain and Australia on 30 October.

But this would prove to be the peak of the stadium's history. Hull did not make it to the First Division as many had expected, and gradually the capacity was reduced owing to the implications of the Taylor Report. In 1982 the North Stand was demolished and replaced with a supermarket, just leaving the front

terrace behind, echoing the fate of Bolton's Railway End at Burnden Park.

The aftermath of the Safety of Sports Ground Act 1985 required major work to be carried out on the ground. This included the closure of the East Stand after terracing at the rear of the stand was categorised as unsafe and this coincided with the ending of the use of the railway link. The East Stand was re-opened with a reduced capacity and in the following three years nearly £600,000 was spent on bringing the stadium up to the new standard. This work included replacing the South Stand terracing and the building of executive boxes at the rear of the West Stand.

The Boothferry Park pitch was totally refurbished before the start of the 1991–92 season, which included the installation of a complete new drainage system. At the same time, the corporate boxes in the West Stand were extended.

Little else was done to Boothferry Park until the continuing poor state of repair of the East Stand covered areas led to its complete closure in 1996. The stand was re-opened in 1997 after the capacity was further reduced and some remedial work had been carried out, but a failure to meet the minimum standards set out in the Taylor Report meant it was closed down again in early 1999. This resulted in Hull City carrying out major reconstruction work on the stand with the financial support of the Football Trust. Problems with the weather and the foundations of the stand caused delays and the stand did not re-open until March 2000.

Throughout the late 1990s and the early part of this century, Hull's fortunes were at their lowest ebb with boardroom battles, administration and ground lockouts, and the club were on the brink of financial collapse. The ground acquired the affectionate nicknames of 'Fer Ark', and 'Bothferry', owing to various damaged signage around the stadium. It was indicative that the ground's best days had gone.

Hull moved out in 2002, taking up residence at the new KC (Kingston Communications) Stadium, to be shared with rugby league side Hull FC. It was there that City reached England's top tier in 2008, suggesting that City's new home's best days are indeed still ahead of it.

The old ground was still used for reserve games after the first team's move until being shut in 2003. Partial demolition of the Boothferry site eventually started on 10 January 2008, over five years after the final game had been played there, and the phase was completed during March. The North Stand and the terracing on the South and East Stands were eventually demolished in January 2010 after years of vandalism and arson attacks, local fire services being called out nearly 100 times during 2009 to deal with the emergencies. The six pylons that had dominated the west Hull skyline were finally dismantled in early 2011.

With confidence returning to the housing sector, work was finally begun in 2013 on building residential homes on the Boothferry Park site. The building works were continuing in 2016, and it is not clear yet if or how the former ground will be commemorated. However the street names on the development, like Legends Way, do in some way reflect its former heritage.

Hull City have boomeranged between the Premier League and the Championship over the last 10 seasons, and were relegated from the top division once again at the end of the 2016–17 season. The new stadium was renamed the KCOM Stadium in April 2016.

Above: Boothferry Park's West Stand in the 1980s.

Left: South Stand, 1989.

Kidderminster Harriers   Aggborough

Address: Hoo Road, Kidderminster, Worcestershire DY10 1NB

Highest attendance: 9,155 v Hereford United, 27 November 1948

First league match: Kidderminster Harriers 2-0 v Torquay United, 12 August 2000

Final league match: Kidderminster Harriers 1-4 v Grimsby Town, 30 April 2005

International matches: England U-19, England U-16

Other usages: Worcester City (2013-2016), West Bromwich Albion U-21

Ground layout: Main Stand, East Stand, The Town End, The College End

Status: Extant

Current stadium: Aggborough

The rather regally named Aggborough finally tasted league football at the second attempt in 2000. The stadium had been rejected six years previously owing to non-compliance with Football League regulations. But it has been home to Kidderminster Harriers since 1890, the club arriving from the nearby White Wickets cricket ground after switching codes from rugby. As the name suggests, they were originally an athletics club and were one of 12 founder members of the Birmingham and District League. Whilst in the Football League, it was the only league ground in Worcestershire.

Aggborough in its early years was nothing more than a pitch with a rope around it, formerly used by United Choirs Rugby Club. Later, the ground was enclosed in an oval shape with a single wooden grandstand on the western touchline and a banked athletics track around the pitch. The club folded in 1891, but Harriers re-formed almost immediately and with athletics also at the ground, it was a very popular venue in the post First World War years.

After the war, the ground was purchased by the Kidderminster Harriers Ground Company Ltd who charged the football club rent to play there, and this problem was not resolved until the council bought the ground in 1945. By then the grandstand had gone, replaced in the 1920s by a corrugated iron Cowshed.

A new 460-seat grandstand was opened in August 1935, and after the Second World War the area in front of this stand was terraced, and the running track replaced by a cycle track. By the Second World War covered areas had been created on the east and southern sides of the ground.

On 27 November 1948 the ground's record attendance of 9,155 was set for an FA Cup first-round replay against Hereford United. In 1951 floodlights were installed, and in 1955 Aggborough became the first ground in England to host a floodlit FA Cup game, when on 14 September in a preliminary round match against Brierley Hill Alliance they won 4–2 in front of 2,230. The initial lights were not a great success, with a new system installed in 1966.

In 1975 the Cowshed roof was demolished in a gale. It was repaired, but the old structure was finally

North Terrace, 1998.

Aggborough's Main Stand, 1998.

Old East Stand, 1994.

replaced in April 1979 by a new East Stand, then called the Bill Greaves Memorial Stand.

In 1983 Kidderminster began making serious waves in non-league football, after promotion to the new Alliance Premier League (the Conference forerunner). Substantial terracing was created all around the pitch and the floodlights were once again upgraded.

In the early 1990s the cycle track was removed completely and identical covered terracing was built on the open areas at each end of the pitch, the College End and the Town End, later called the North Terrace and the South Terrace. It was the beginning of a long-term redevelopment of the ground, and a new Main Stand was under construction in 1994.

Unfortunately, the Harriers' success came more quickly than expected. When promotion was achieved as champions five years later, the ground was not complete owing to an extended FA Cup run and their place in the Football League was denied due to the tightened fire safety regulations.

Ironically, the ground had hosted an 8,000 crowd without any problems for the visit of Premier League West Ham United in the fifth round of the FA Cup that year. Aggborough's main stand was of wooden construction, and despite the new cantilever stand being completed on time, complying with all regulations, and despite considerable West Midlands media support, the Football League rejected Harriers' promotion. It was a very controversial decision, as many existing grounds already in use in the Third Division possessed facilities that were nowhere near as good as those at Aggborough.

Six seasons later the club were ready when they were Conference champions again in 2000, and league football finally arrived at Aggborough. Then in 2003, they built the ground's focal point – a new single tiered, cantilever East Stand that could seat over 2,000 spectators and which cost over £1 million, bringing the total redevelopment costs to over £2 million. Perspex panels had been incorporated into the front of its roof allowing sunlight to reach the pitch.

Sadly, success was rather ephemeral and the Harriers were relegated back to the Conference in 2005, and spent the next 11 seasons there, only once looking in contention to return. Financial problems mounted, and the club's debts had spiralled to £250,000 by 2010. Loyal fans raised £150,000 to keep the club afloat. At the end of 2015–16, the club were demoted again to the National League North, but are currently looking forward to a quick return, reaching the play-offs in 2016–17.

Worcester City shared the Aggborough ground with Kidderminster for three seasons from 2013–14.

Below: The old Main Stand in the 1970s.

Leicester City

Address: Filbert Street, Leicester LE2 7JG

Highest attendance: 47,298 v Tottenham Hotspur (FA Cup), 18 February 1928

First league match: Leicester City 4-2 v Rotherham Town, 8 September 1894

Final league match: Leicester City 2-1 v Tottenham Hotspur, 11 May 2002

Ground layout: Main Stand/Carling Stand, North Stand/Filbert Street End, South Stand/ Spion Kop, East Stand/Popular Side

Status: Demolished

Current stadium: The King Power Stadium

Leicester City played at Filbert Street, nestled in the middle of densely-populated terraced housing, from 1891 until 2002 after having inhabited a number of different grounds in the first seven years of their history. Leicester Fosse became a professional club in 1889 and laid out its own ground at Mill Lane, just north of Filbert Street.

The club was soon forced to move, however, as the local corporation requested the land for development. The site of what was to become Filbert Street was prepared during the summer of 1891. The club joined the Second Division of the Football League in 1894–95.

For its early years Leicester Fosse were residents, but the club was wound up following the First World War. Newly-formed Leicester City took their place in 1919, though historians consider both clubs to be the same.

It was only after the Fosse era that the ground began to take shape. The ground initially consisted of simple earth banks and a small main stand on the west side until 1921, when a new and much larger Main Stand was built, eventually complete with a 'pigeon loft'.

Six years later this was followed by a double-decker South Stand (known as the Spion Kop), built by Leitch, culminating in Filbert Street's record attendance in 1928. It became generally known as 'the double-decker'. Originally this was built with seating above and terracing below. The old roof from the South Stand was transferred to the North (Filbert Street End). The middle section of the Main Stand suffered bomb damage in November 1940, and was later further damaged by a serious fire. By 1949 the stand had been rebuilt, with much of the labour, ironically, being supplied by German POWs from a nearby camp. Also at this time the open East Stand/ Popular Side was covered.

Floodlights were installed and first used for a match against German club Borussia Dortmund in October 1957. After just surviving an earlier council vote to terminate their lease in the late 1940s, City purchased the freehold of the ground in 1962, for the sum of £30,500.

In 1971 the first moves towards an all-seater stadium were taken, as the North and East sides were converted to seating. In that same year City pioneered a method introduced to protect the pitch using a polythene cover. The 'Air Dome' covered an area of 90,000 square feet, weighed over a ton and took 15 men two hours to lay out and inflate using four electric fans. The experiment lasted 11 years. In 1975, 20 basic executive boxes were added to the top of the North Stand replacing the old roof.

Below: The Filbert Street End, 1979.

Opposite left: The East Stand/Popular Side, 1989.

Opposite right: Spion Kop/South Stand.

At the beginning of the 1990s, after considering both a move to a new stadium as well as a total redevelopment of Filbert Street which would have seen the pitch rotated by 90 degrees on to the car park behind the Main Stand, City opted instead to build a new Main Stand, demolishing the existing structure in the summer of 1992. Completed in December 1993, the two-tiered Carling Stand costing £6 million held nearly 10,000 seated spectators and was equipped with expanded corporate facilities.

In 1994 the final terraced 'Kop' area was converted to seating giving Filbert Street an all-seated capacity of 21,500 and bringing it into compliance with the Taylor Report.

A sustained period of top-flight success in the late 1990s saw the club consider relocation, and just four years after the erection of the Carling Stand, the club decided to move to a purpose-built stadium to provide for higher attendances and to give better facilities.

The expansion of Filbert Street would have been very difficult, as the North and East Stands backed directly on to housing. Manager Martin O'Neill described Filbert Street at the time as 'one fantastic stand, one adequate one, and the other two parts are Vauxhall Conference'!

The club purchased Freeman's Wharf, a former power station site 200 yards south of Filbert Street. Work began on a 32,500-seater stadium and it was opened in the summer of 2002. At the time, the stadium was named in conjunction with the sponsors, Walkers Crisps.

Filbert Street was sold to a development company for £3.75 million in March 2002. The last game to be played at Filbert Street was on the 11 May 2002, a 2–1 victory over Tottenham Hotspur.

Demolition of Filbert Street began in March 2003. Part of the site is now home to the 'Filbert Village' development, built as accommodation for students of the nearby De Montfort University and University of Leicester. The road running through the development is called Lineker Road, named after one of Leicester City's most famous players. The Carling Stand was demolished only nine years after its construction.

The rest of the site was meant to be developed for housing, but this work was cancelled due to the national financial crisis of 2007–08. It was then leased to a car parking company, but this arrangement was terminated by Leicester City Council in March 2012. Sadly, half of the former ground is now just neglected boarded-up scrubland and an open area for less-caring folk to dispose of all manner of unwanted household items and rubbish. The eyesore does no credit to the exciting times that have gone before.

Success was not immediate at their new home as City dropped into League One for the first time in their history in 2008, climbing back the next year and advancing to the play-offs in 2010. They were beaten in the play-offs again in 2013, but returned to the Premier League as champions the following year. After a year of consolidation, they achieved the pinnacle of success with the unlikely but very popular Premier League title in 2015–16. The naming rights of the new stadium were sold to King Power at the start of the 2011–12 season.

Lincoln City

Address: Sincil Bank Stadium, Lincoln, Lincolnshire LN5 8LD

Highest attendance: 23,196 v Derby County (League Cup), 15 November 1967

First league match: Lincoln City 1–1 v Woolwich Arsenal, 14 September 1895

Final league match: Lincoln City 0–3 v Aldershot Town, 07 May 2011

International matches: England U-16

Other usages: Rock Concerts

Ground layout: Sincil Bank/Co-op Stand, South Park Stand/Bridge McFarlane Stand, Railway End/Stacey West Stand, St Andrews Stand/Main Stand, Family Stand

Status: Extant

Current stadium: Sincil Bank

Right: South Park Stand and new Co-op Community Stand, 1997.

Opposite: Stacey West Stand, 1993.

By 1884 there were a host of clubs in the area, including Lincoln Cricket and Football Club, Rangers, Albion and newly formed Lincoln Rovers, the originally named Lincoln Recreation. The formation of Lincoln City was to create a team from Lincoln capable of competing for the Lincolnshire Senior Cup. Lincoln City had several fields to choose from and a new pitch was found at John O' Gaunts, preferred because it provided the option of enclosing the venue and hence charging entrance fee money.

Meanwhile the gentlemen from Lindum FC, increasingly worried by the new team in town, approached Lincoln City with a merger plan but the proposal was rejected. In an effort to effectively kill Lincoln City, Lindum FC moved to Sincil Drain, slightly northwards from today's Sincil Bank but still the origin of the present ground. However, Lincoln City's good fortunes on the field since joining the inaugural season of the Second Division in 1892–93 eventually forced Lindum to succumb to defeat. Their vacant pitch was taken over by Lincoln City in the summer of 1895 and they developed it into what is now Sincil Bank.

The first match at the new ground was a goalless friendly against Gainsborough Trinity, and Woolwich Arsenal provided the opposition for the first league game which took place on 14 September 1895.

In the summer of 1896 a small, uncovered stand was built at the South Park End, turnstiles were added, and the rope surrounding the pitch was replaced with wire. The ground was more fully developed between 1898 and 1902 with the help of the Working Men's Committee. Extensive banking was added around the field, and in the summer of 1899 a covered stand holding around 400 was built on the Sincil Bank side; this was known then as the Working Men's Stand.

In 1901 another stand was built behind the South Park goal, with the existing structure moved to the south-east corner alongside the main grandstand. In 1902 the St Andrews Stand along the eastern side

was enlarged and moved back to allow a permanent cycling and athletics track to be laid down in front of it.

The Working Men's Committee made small improvements every summer, adding turnstiles, extra banking, and new dressing rooms with plunge and shower baths. In February 1908 a section of the stand on the St Andrews side was destroyed by a storm which uprooted the supports, and five spectators required hospital treatment.

By 1915 the ground consisted of three covered stands on the St Andrews, South Park, and Sincil Bank sides, with banking around the remaining areas to provide a better view for those who chose to stand up. The ground survived the Great War intact, and when the club's finances improved in the mid-1920s further improvements were made. This was despite the fact that the club had been demoted from the Football League three times between 1908 and 1920, playing in regional leagues.

In 1925, with the club now back in the league in the newly-formed Third Division North, a small shelter was built at the centre of the Railway End, partly paid for by the supporters' club which had established a fund to raise £1,200 to cover the whole of the north side of the ground, and most of the work was carried out by the Working Men's Committee.

The area under the South Park Stand was also developed at this time with new offices for the secretary, a boardroom, and a gymnasium. A wooden fence was put up around the perimeter of the pitch which had previously been wired off. By the late 1920s there was clearly a need for major improvements, particularly to the grandstands which dated from the turn of the century, but the club's position as yearly tenants made the board reluctant to act.

In September 1929 the South Park Stand was completely gutted by fire which also destroyed the offices and all the club records. A new wood and brick structure seating 1,500 was erected within six weeks and was used for the first time for the visit of Carlisle United on 16 November. Shortly afterwards

the ground was purchased from a Colonel Swann for £4,875. Ownership gave the directors the confidence to proceed with modernising the stadium and fundamental changes were made over the next few years.

In the summer of 1931 the covered area at the Railway End was extended by adding a second small shelter, and terracing was laid down. In the following close season the St Andrews Stand was demolished to be replaced by a new structure with a capacity of 2,250 in a small seated enclosure and a small bank of terracing at the front. At the same time concrete terracing was laid down in front of both this and the South Park Stand.

Sincil Bank was requisitioned by the ARP services for the duration of the Second World War, but despite all efforts it fell in to a state of disrepair. When peace returned, money was readily available for improvements, but resources were scarce.

Sufficient concrete blocks were obtained to replace the fencing around the pitch with a wall behind the two goals in 1945, and this was extended to the St Andrews and Sincil Bank sides 12 months later. In 1947 the ARP cleansing station was converted to modern dressing rooms and the old wooden structure demolished and removed. The capacity of the ground was increased to 25,000 in 1948 when the Sincil Bank Stand, which was in a poor state of repair, was demolished and the wood from it was used to create a bank of shale terracing.

From the 1950s the ground was developed further through the donations of the supporters' club. Concrete terracing was laid down on the Sincil Bank side during the 1952–53 season and by the end of the decade, the 'Spion Kop' area in the north-east corner had been concreted over and covered with a shelter.

Proposals by the club to build a new stand linking the St Andrews and South Park structures were discussed in detail in the mid-1950s but never came to fruition. The field at the rear of the St Andrews Stand was purchased in 1955 and this was used for training and as a venue for reserve team fixtures.

Floodlighting was installed in 1962, again paid for by the supporters' club, and used for the first time on 31 January against Barnsley. Two years later a social club was opened beneath the South Park Stand, but the 1960s were generally a period of decline and financial crisis for the club, being relegated to the Fourth Division in 1962–63. They began to emerge from this position towards the end of the decade and the replayed League Cup tie against Derby County in November 1967 attracted a new record attendance of 23,196.

In September 1975 the wall behind the South Park goal collapsed during a League Cup match with Stoke City, and this section of terracing was never used again. The original floodlights were replaced with a new and more powerful set in February 1977, with the old lights being sold to Spalding United. The club made considerable progress during the period, gaining promotion under future Watford and England manager Graham Taylor.

Following a substantial loss in the 1981–82 season the directors sold the ground to the City Council for £225,000 to ensure the future of league football in Lincoln. The original agreement was for a 21-year lease but this was extended to 125 years shortly after.

With a ground dating from the early 1930s, and two stands principally of timber construction, urgent work was needed at Sincil Bank following the Bradford disaster. The South Park Stand was closed to spectators for the 1985–86 campaign but was then reopened during the following season after the St Andrews Stand had been demolished in the summer of 1986. This was the prelude to the final period of redevelopment of the ground.

The club though had received a double blow of successive relegations, leading to them being relegated from the Football League in May 1987. The first stage of this recovery saw a new St Andrews Stand seating 1,400 opened in November 1987.

It was smaller in size than originally envisaged, partly due to the club's single-season drop into Conference football. Running only half the length of the pitch, it held the press box and directors' enclosure. This was in addition to the majority of the club's offices and corporate areas. It would be generally known in later years as the Main Stand.

The South Park and Railway Ends were both demolished in the early months of 1990 and in August of the same year the Stacey West Stand – named after two long-serving City fans who tragically died in the Bradford fire – was opened at the Railway End of the ground. The rail goods line that ran behind the stand had been dismantled in the same year.

Sincil Bank side, 1993, before the new Co-op Community Stand.

This stand originally had areas of terracing at either end with a large area of seating in between so that supporters had choice. However, when Lincoln were promoted to the old Division Two at the end of the 1997–98 season, the stand was made entirely terraced. When the club was relegated back to the old Division Three the following season, a grant by the Football Trust partially enabled almost 2,000 seats to be purchased to totally replace the terracing which meant that Sincil Bank, for the first time in its history, was an all-seater stadium.

A new South Park Stand with 17 executive boxes was operational in the summer of 1992. The separate Family Stand appeared alongside the St Andrews Stand in 1994, previously occupied by a small, open terrace, and is commonly known as Poacher's Corner.

The final stage of the redevelopment saw the completion of the single-tier 5,700 seat Linpave Stand in March 1995 on the Sincil Bank side. This was the largest stand at Sincil Bank. It cost around £1 million to build, and is more commonly known today as the Co-op Community Stand.

A modern floodlighting system was also installed at this time. The total cost of rebuilding the ground amounted to around £3 million, with significant contributions coming from both the city council and the Football Trust. This meant that the ground had a capacity of over 10,000 and was arguably one of the best stadiums in lower league football.

In March 2000 the club decided to buy back the ground with the city council agreeing to a knock-down sale price of £175,000, meaning that the club could use the all-seater stadium as collateral as they sought to relieve another financial crisis. This crisis led to the club going into administration in May 2002.

On a weekend in May 2006 the Irish pop band Westlife and other supporting acts including Liberty X, Blue's Lee Ryan and Journey South performed in front of over 13,000 fans at Sincil Bank

The Main Stand/St Andrews Stand, 1993.

– the biggest concert ever to take place in the city of Lincoln.

On 28 November 2008 Sincil Bank hosted England U-16s 2–0 win over Scotland U-16s to win the Victory Shield, an annual football competition between the four home nations at the Under-16 level.

Over the years the ground has hosted many different events including a visit from Queen Elizabeth II in June 1958, and a major pop concert in May 1966 featuring groups such as The Who, The Kinks and The Small Faces. Gainsborough Trinity have also used Sincil Bank on a couple of occasions for games when

the Northolme was unavailable. Local cricket and football finals, boxing, wrestling, athletics, cycling, grass tennis, and American football have all taken place at the venue at one time or another.

Sadly, the Imps lost their league status again in 2011 and have since competed in the Conference. However, after a very successful 2016–17 campaign which culminated in the team becoming the first non-league side to reach the quarter-finals of the FA Cup in over 100 years, Lincoln City returned to the Football League as champions of the Vanarama National League.

Macclesfield Town

Moss Rose

Address: Moss Rose Stadium, London Road, Macclesfield, Cheshire SK11 7SP

Highest attendance: 9,003 v Winsford United (Cheshire Cup), 14 February 1948

First league match: Macclesfield Town 2-1 v Torquay United, 9 August 1997

Final league match: Macclesfield Town 0-2 v Burton Albion, 28 April 2012

Ground-sharing: Chester City

Ground layout: Main Stand, Alfred McAlpine Stand, Star Lane Stand, Silkman End

Status: Extant

Current stadium: Moss Rose

Below: Star Lane Terrace and Estate Road Side, 1998.

Opposite: Main Stand, 1998.

In September 1891 the club moved from Bowfield Lane to their present home at Moss Rose, despite critics who objected to the proximity of a public house! However, within two years they were declared bankrupt. An amateur club, Hallifield moved into Moss Rose in 1897 and joined the Manchester District League, adopting the name Macclesfield in 1902. Whilst the club was in the Football League it was the second oldest ground in the four divisions. Macclesfield have always been a top non-league side, but also one that has survived several financial crises, especially in the mid-1930s and mid-1970s.

The ground began to take shape around 1906 when a timber stand was erected on the main road which at that stage had a grass bank all around. On 6 October the 'New Grandstand' was opened. It is not known when the old dressing rooms were built in the pub corner of the ground, but most likely around this time. Also, slightly later, two areas of cover were put up along most of the terrace opposite the stand.

When competitive football resumed after the Second World War, Macclesfield Town Football Club Ltd was formed and the club gained their current name. They joined the Cheshire County League in 1946–47. On 14 February 1948 Moss Rose achieved its highest gate of 9,003 against Winsford United in the second round of the Cheshire Senior Cup.

The first floodlighting system was installed for the start of the 1965–66 season. The first match under the lights was played on 1 September 1965 against Northwich Victoria, Macclesfield winning 4–1. Malcolm Allison and Sir Stanley Matthews performed the official opening.

In the summer of 1968 the old grandstand which had served the club for over 60 years was replaced at a cost of £14,000 by the impressive cantilevered structure which exists today. It had a 650-seat capacity and has since been developed at the back with various offices, and also houses the dressing rooms; this is known as the Main Stand, or the London Road side or the Silk FM Main Stand.

This stand was covered with a raised seating area, which meant that spectators had to ascend a small staircase to enter it. It had windshields to either side and ran for about a third of the length of the pitch, straddling the halfway line. This type of stand was a classic design, once common across the country. It had portions of terracing to each side and at its front. The team dugouts were also located on this side.

That same year, the club became founder members of the Northern Premier League (NPL) after winning their final Cheshire League title. The club became inaugural winners of the league. Then the following season they retained the title and added another first to the record books, as FA Trophy winners at Wembley in 1970. During this period and after, Macclesfield Town were considered one of the finest

non-league sides in the country, and promotion to the Conference was achieved after winning their third NPL title in 1986–87.

The ground gained further terracing at one end and around the stand in 1988, removing all the grass banking in the process. There were also new offices and changing rooms. A new social club was opened in 1990.

Between 1990 and 1992 Chester City, members of the old Third Division, played two seasons of 'home' matches at the Moss Rose whilst their new Deva stadium was being built. Being shared, the Moss Rose pitch had to contend with more than 50 first-team matches a season from the two sides.

Following Macclesfield's Conference win at the end of the 1994–95 season, the Football League announced that Moss Rose was unsuitable for staging league football. This was very controversial as Moss Rose had been deemed fit for league football only three years earlier after only minor alterations that had allowed Chester City to ground share.

This was explained away by the FA as a 'tightening of the regulations' that had occurred during those intervening years. This led to a number of improvements at the ground which proved fruitful when Macclesfield finally won promotion to the Football League in 1997.

Part of this improvement programme that year was to purchase seats from the Ayresome Park auction at Middlesbrough for the Star Lane End, put in to achieve the mandatory number in order to climb out of the Conference. Also known as The Macclesfield Audi Stand, this former open and now covered stand was unusual in that it was a mix of seating and terracing, having a terraced area behind the seating area. This end was for home supporters. More recently, the club bought more seats from Stoke's old Victoria Ground to replace sections of the Main Stand.

The first ever league match played at the Moss Rose was on 9 August 1997 against Torquay United,

Macclesfield winning 2–1. Incredibly, Macclesfield won promotion as runners up in their inaugural year. On gaining promotion to the Second Division in 1998, the old Estate Road terrace was replaced with a temporary 1,700-seater stand. The promotion proved to be a step too far and the Silkmen returned to the basement at the end of that season.

On 5 May 2001 the new permanent all-seater Alfred McAlpine Stand with hospitality on the Estate Road side built at a cost of around £1.5 million was opened by former manager Sammy McIlroy.

At the opposite end was the open John Askey terrace (Silkman End) named after a former player/ current manager, which was given to away supporters. At some stage there were plans to cover this and add some seats at the rear and also build a leisure complex and hotel behind it, but the finances required to do this have yet to be found.

In September 2007 the club had hoped to move to a new stadium as part of a wider project to regenerate Macclesfield town centre which had been backed by Cheshire East Council. These regeneration plans had included the provision of a new 7,000 capacity stadium, situated south of the town centre, just a mile away from Moss Rose. However, the scheme lost momentum and although 70 per cent of those questioned were supportive of the scheme, objections were raised as to whether the council should be spending money on a stadium, so the club remained at Moss Rose.

In May 2012 after 15 seasons competing in the Football League, Macclesfield finished the season in basement position resulting in relegation (for only the second time in the club's history), to the Conference thereby returning to the non-league scene. Since that time the Silkmen have remained comfortably placed in the Vanarama National League, without seemingly threatening an imminent return to league football.

Maidstone United

Name: Watling Street (Dartford)

Highest attendance: 5,538 v Cambridge United, 16 May 1990

First league match: Maidstone United 4–1 v Scarborough, 26 August 1989

Final league match: Maidstone United 0–0 v Mansfield Town, 25 April 1992

Ground layout: Main Stand, East Terrace, Watling Street End, North Stand

Status: Demolished

Current stadium: The Gallagher Stadium

Below: The Watling Street End, 1989.

Of all the grounds contained in this book this, in some ways, is the cuckoo in the nest. Although it deals with the brief flame that was Maidstone United, it is as much to do with Dartford, as for their entire lifetime in the Football League, Maidstone United ground-shared and played their home games at a venue which was not their own. The arrangement finally had dire consequences for both clubs.

Dartford FC bought five acres of land for £1,000 in Watling Street in 1921. A large, seated grandstand was built on the western touchline at a cost of £3,000 with banking installed around the rest of the pitch. The stand opened on 19 November. However the stand didn't last long. In February 1926 it was destroyed along with the dressing rooms, boardroom and offices by a fire. The club had not taken out any insurance so they had to start a fund to replace the destroyed facility.

In March 1927 a new steel constructed 1,000-seater stand was officially opened, and three years later a covered enclosure was built down the opposite east side. There were no further changes during the 1930s and the ground thankfully didn't suffer at the hands of Luftwaffe during the Second World War.

In 1946 the club laid terracing at the Watling Street End of the ground (South) and later in front of the western Main Stand. Over the decades there were general improvements to all sides of the ground, and in October 1963 Dartford installed floodlights at a cost of £6,000. During the 1970s, the supporters' association was extremely active and made further improvements to the ground and its surroundings. This period saw Watling Street at its peak, an old-fashioned football venue which generated an excellent atmosphere.

In the wake of the Hillsborough and Bradford disasters, Dartford, like so many clubs, had to upgrade their facilities or move; they decided on the former. Large sums of money were spent on planning and design fees, which burdened a manageable financial deficit with crippling interest charges. At the same time Maidstone United, on the verge of their finest hour winning the Conference in 1988–89, had sold their own large, bowl-shaped site at the Athletic Ground in London Road to a furniture chain for £3 million. The thinking behind this was that their current stadium was in need of repair and not large enough for league football. Promotion to the Fourth Division of the Football League duly arrived with Maidstone United homeless.

Needing a suitable venue to launch their foray into the Football League, the Dartford board agreed to let Maidstone ground-share. An upgraded new Main Stand was built at Watling Street to house Maidstone's fans and the ground was refurbished. However, the 40-mile round trip distance caused average attendances to eventually fall from around 2,400 to 1,400.

After a shaky start in their first season in the Fourth Division, Maidstone reached the promotion play-offs but lost to eventual winners Cambridge United in a dramatic two-leg semi-final; the game saw the ground's record attendance. Their form in the following season went from very good to very poor in a short period of time; the club were lurching into serious financial problems as they had spent vast amounts getting into the Football League and the spending had continued now that they were there.

The club then took a massive gamble, and without any kind of planning permission, purchased a piece of land east of Maidstone for £400,000 with a view to building a 10,000 capacity ground on it with a sports complex. With a ground in the town, the club believed they would be able to afford to continue in the Football League. However, the gamble did not pay off and the planning application to build on the land, which included a retail park, was turned down by the council.

During the 1991–92 season, the club and the players were put up for sale. But with huge debts, no ground and a poor team, there was little interest. Somehow they survived the season, but as the new season approached it looked less and less likely that the Stones would be able to play in it as their financial worries showed no sign of easing and the debts had reached £650,000.

On top of this, the Watling Street ground at which the club had been playing had also ended up being in dire need of renovation work which was going to prove costly. Additionally, the installation of seats behind one goal at Watling Street had been carried out without planning permission, leading to more money being spent and wasted on an area of the ground that stayed closed and empty.

The Stones were due to play their first game of the season at Scunthorpe United, but by this stage only two players were still registered to the club. The Watling Street stadium had now just been sold, leaving Maidstone United without a home and not knowing where they would be playing their home games even if they remained in existence. The match was cancelled.

The club were given 48 hours to guarantee that they would be able to fulfil their fixtures. Unable to come up with the necessary backing, they resigned from the Football League on 17 August and went into liquidation owing almost £1 million.

Ground improvement costs, which Maidstone United had paid for, had been passed back to Dartford for around half a million pounds which had pushed their own debts far beyond manageable proportions. Sadly this had left only one option open.

Watling Street was necessarily sold off to repay creditors which had forced Dartford themselves to withdraw from the Southern League four games into the 1992–93 season. The stadium was razed to the ground almost immediately and housing was built on the land.

After 14 long years in exile, ground-sharing at various venues, the re-formed Dartford FC moved into Princes Park on 11 November 2006. The new stadium is one of the best in non-league football, although some older fans still regret the loss of Watling Street. The club currently participates in the National League South, the sixth tier of English football.

From the nucleus of their youth team, Maidstone United themselves were re-formed in 1993 as Maidstone Invicta, a name they held for four years before re-taking the name United. They led a nomadic existence for 20 years working their way up the non-league pyramid, but returned to Maidstone in 2012 for the first time since 1988 with their first match at their new home, the £2.6 million Gallagher Stadium.

Maidstone gained a second successive promotion to the Vanarama National League in 2016, bringing fifth-tier football back to the town for the first time since the old club was promoted to the Football League. So there are now strong hopes that one day league football may return to Maidstone, this time better financed and with their own stadium.

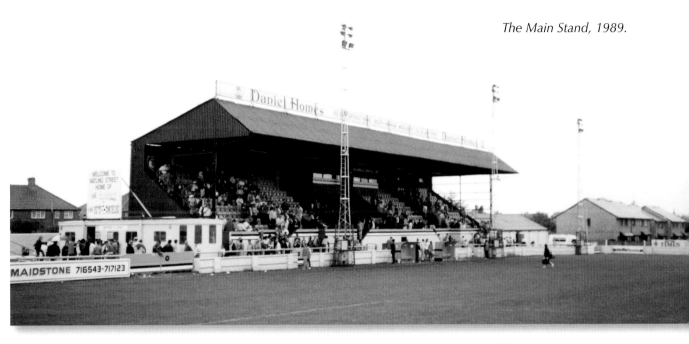

The Main Stand, 1989.

Manchester City
Maine Road

Address: Moss Side, Manchester M14 7WN

Highest attendance: 84,569 v Stoke City (FA Cup), 3 March 1934

First league match: Manchester City 2-1 v Sheffield United, 25 August 1923

Final league match: Manchester City 0-1 v Southampton, 11 May 2003

International matches: England (1943 to 1949)

Other usages: FA Cup semi-finals, Football League Cup Final, FA Charity Shield matches, Rugby League Championship finals, Rock Concerts

Ground-sharing: Manchester United (1945-49)

Ground layout: Main Stand, North Stand/Scoreboard End, Platt Lane End/Umbro Stand, Popular Side/Kippax Stand

Status: Demolished

Current stadium: The City of Manchester Stadium (Eastlands) (The Etihad Stadium)

Right: The Popular Side, 1967.

Home to Manchester City before the club was a prince (though it was hardly a pauper), Maine Road was once the largest club ground in the country, breaking attendance records in both league and FA Cup games. City joined the Second Division in 1893–94 and left a cramped and fire-damaged Hyde Road in 1923 to take up residence at a ground with an initial estimated capacity of 80–100,000, consisting of mainly terracing, and a Main Stand capable of holding 10,000 even though it didn't even extend the full length of the pitch. It quickly earned the title of the 'Wembley of the North'.

A 16-acre former brickworks on Maine Road was purchased for £5,500, and Maine Road was originally known as Dog Kennel Lane but renamed Maine Road (after the Maine law) during the 1870s at the insistence of the Temperance Movement who owned land on Dog Kennel Lane, and the local authority accepted their request.

The initial layout of the ground consisted of the one covered Main Stand, and uncovered terracing on the other three sides, with gentle curves connecting the corners. The construction cost was £100,000. At the time, it had the largest roof span of any stand at any football ground in the country.

The first match at Maine Road took place on 25 August 1923 when 58,159 fans watched the home side beat Sheffield United 2–1. The first changes to the ground took place in 1931, when the corner between the Main Stand and the Platt Lane End at the south of the ground was rebuilt to incorporate a roof and the installation of benches. This renovation was to be the first of many.

In 1934 the second highest attendance at an English football game at a club ground was recorded

The North Stand, 1967.

The Main Stand, 2000.

at Maine Road; this was between Manchester City and Stoke City in front of 84,569 fans in the sixth round of the FA Cup on 3 March. Queues formed four hours before the match and Maine Road was packed and turnstiles closed two hours before kick-off. The match was won 1–0 by Manchester City.

Further changes at the Platt Lane End took place in 1935, extending the terracing and providing a roof for the full stand. This marked the peak capacity of the ground, estimated at around 88,000. Further changes were planned, but suspended when Manchester City were relegated from the First Division in 1938, and abandoned entirely when the Second World War broke out.

The stadium was shared by Manchester United after the Second World War as their Old Trafford ground had been damaged during the Manchester blitz. The highest attendance for a league game at Maine Road occurred during this period, when 83,260 people watched Manchester United play Arsenal on 17 January 1948. This figure is a national record for a league game.

Maine Road also hosted three England internationals at that time: the first was a war-time international and it witnessed England's 8–0 demolition of Scotland on 16 October 1943; the second was a 3–0 defeat of Wales on 13 November 1946 and the third a 9–2 win over Northern Ireland on 16 November 1949, England's first-ever World Cup qualifier.

Floodlights were installed in 1953, and in 1957, prompted by the hosting of two FA Cup semi-finals in successive years, the side facing the Main Stand (which until that time was generally known as the Popular Side) was extended and roofed and named The Kippax Stand after a nearby street.

In 1963 several rows of benches were installed at the Platt Lane End, meaning that Maine Road had more seats than any other English club ground of the time. A year later the floodlights were replaced with much higher and more powerful floodlight towers. In 1967 improvements were made to the Main Stand roof; the middle section of the roof was replaced by a rather odd-looking construction which allowed an

unhindered view for the directors and those in the most expensive seats, but it did little to improve the look of the stadium.

The next major redevelopment came in the 1970s, with the construction of the 8,000 capacity North Stand, a cantilevered stand which remained in place until the closure of Maine Road. Initially the stand was terracing, but after a year the management decided to turn it into a seated stand.

The 1980s saw ambitious plans for improvements; however, these plans were shelved due to financial pressures after the Main Stand roof had been replaced again, this time with a distinctive cream-coloured barrel affair held up by two enormous stanchions, at a cost of £1 million.

By 1990 it was apparent that some areas of the ground were becoming outdated, and there was the need for the stadium to become all-seater, so in 1991 seats in the front section of the North Stand were replaced and a year later the Platt Lane End stand was demolished. Its place was taken by the two-tier, all-seater Umbro Stand that also incorporated 48

Top: The Kippax Stand, 2000.

Above: Maine Road's Platt Lane End, 1970s.

executive boxes; it cost £6 million and was opened in March 1993. The stand's name reverted to the Platt Lane Stand in 1997.

The era of standing accommodation at Maine Road came to an end in May 1994 as the stadium became all-seater with the demolition of the Kippax Street Terrace. A three-tier stand was built in its place, holding nearly 14,000 spectators, and on its completion in October 1995 it was the tallest stand in the country. It was built at a cost of £16 million, four times the turnover of the club according to the chairman.

The revamp of the Kippax was the second phase of a five-part development plan that would have cost £40 million. The board had recognised that the rest of the ground needed serious improvement, and the new stand had emphasised the haphazard nature in which the ground had been redeveloped, as all four sides were of differing heights and construction styles.

The board made dramatic and impressive plans to reconstruct the rest of the ground, extending the other three sides of the ground to allow for a construction similar to the new Kippax, giving a total capacity of around 50,000. However, the club abandoned these as City were relegated from the Premier League in 1996 and from Division One two years later.

Instead just a temporary stand, nicknamed the Gene Kelly Stand as fans became accustomed to 'singing in the rain', was erected in the corner between the Kippax and the North Stand during the 1997–98 season. This still could not satisfy the huge demand for tickets, and so additional temporary seating was added in stages over the course of the following two seasons.

Whilst not having a small ground, City were still very keen to relocate, and they capitalised on the Commonwealth Games coming to Manchester when they agreed a deal to occupy the 48,000-capacity City of Manchester Stadium in 2002, originally constructed for that occasion. An auction of the ground's fixtures and fittings took place in July 2003, raising £100,000,

which was donated to community projects in the Moss Side area, which was undergoing a lengthy regeneration process. There was interest from clubs such as Preston North End and Norwich City for the bigger lots which could be re-used.

There were various proposals put forward to save the ground as a sports stadium; however, none of them came to fruition. Demolition began in late 2003 and lasted around 10 months, meaning the £16 million Kippax Stand was redundant after just eight years. Two years later, the go-ahead was given for a new housing development to be built on the site.

Maine Road in its day had hosted concerts by many famous artists including Bryan Adams, Bon Jovi, David Bowie, Dire Straits, Fleetwood Mac, Guns 'N Roses, Jean Michel Jarre, The New Power Generation, Pink Floyd, Prince, Queen, The Rolling Stones and Simple Minds. The most high profile concert held at Maine Road was that of Mancunian band Oasis (themselves avowed Manchester City fans) in April 1996, a performance which was later released as a video, *There and Then*.

A new urban village with its own community centre with around 230 houses and 240 apartments was built on the site, the development designed to 'seamlessly integrate into the existing street fabric and provide a catalyst for regeneration of the area.' The development contained a public art display commemorating the stadium and it featured a circular plate half open, symbolising the centre spot and the new development. The club settled at their new venue on a renegotiated 250-year lease from Manchester City Council. Their fortunes have skyrocketed following the takeover by Abu Dhabi billionaire Sheikh Mansour making City the richest club in the world. The stadium was renamed the Etihad Stadium by the club in July 2011 as part of a 10-year sponsorship agreement with the team kit sponsors Etihad Airways.

With such riches available, City have since twice won the coveted domestic Premier League title, but have yet to dominate Europe.

Middlesbrough   Ayresome Park

Address: Ayresome Park Road, Middlesbrough TS5 6BF

Highest attendance: 53,802 v Newcastle United, 27 December 1949

First league match: Middlesbrough 2-3 v Sunderland, 12 September 1903

Final league match: Middlesbrough 2-1 v Luton Town, 30 April 1995

International matches: The World Cup (1966)

Ground layout: North Stand, South Stand, East Stand, West Stand

Status: Demolished

Current stadium: Riverside Stadium

Right: East End Terrace, 1964.

Below: South Stand and West End, 1973.

Ayresome Park was Middlesbrough's sixth home in their 27-year history when they took up residence in 1903. It was built at Paradise Field, adjacent to the old Paradise Ground of Middlesbrough Ironopolis, who had played in the Football League in the 1893–94 season. After turning professional in 1899 the club was elected to the First Division in 1902.

The club had brought the Main Stand from their former home at Linthorpe Road and deposited it at Ayresome Park on the south side. Tons of earth were moved by horse-drawn wagons to build embankments at the east and west ends of the ground, providing terracing for thousands. The ends were initially known as the Linthorpe Road End and the Workhouse End.

The ground's only other covered stand at the time was the barrel-roofed North Stand opposite, meaning that Ayresome was capable of holding 40,000 fans. The stand was designed and built by Archibald Leitch and cost almost £10,500, an enormous sum at the time. It had a characteristic clock at the centre. Work continued throughout the summer of 1903 with the

ground being enclosed by a wooden fence, bringing the total cost, largely financed by loans, to almost £12,000.

The South Stand would be demolished and rebuilt in 1937, while shelter was created for the goal-side West End. Floodlights were installed in 1957. The stadium then became covered on all four sides in preparation for Ayresome being a host venue for the 1966 World Cup; the East Stand was covered and provided seating for 4,000, with additional seats installed in the North and South Stands.

Despite Middlesbrough being a Third Division side at the time, it was a tribute to Ayresome Park that it was hosting such elite games. Three games were played at the ground, involving the Soviet Union, North Korea, Italy and Chile. But the improvements were in hindsight unnecessary; the ground had the lowest attendances of the tournament, and the stadium would remain largely unchanged after that.

On 12 January 1980 tragedy struck when a portion of the ground collapsed following a game with Manchester United. A brick pillar crumbled bringing two gates down with it, killing two people who were Middlesbrough season-ticket holders. It was the start of a terrible trend in football for the coming decade.

Middlesbrough famously had to play their first home game of the 1986–87 season at Hartlepool because they were locked out of Ayresome Park by the bailiffs due to huge debts which almost put the club out of business. However, they were soon back at their home venue after a takeover deal saved the club. Despite this crisis, a £1.2 million sports centre was opened at the stadium on 3 March 1986 after a six-year delay caused by fire and safety regulations.

The bright red roofs on its four stands gave the venue a unique character, while its orderly layout, with the uncovered corners of the stadium neatly curving round to join the stands, was in keeping with football's elite.

Even so, the stadium needed extensive renovation by the 1990s to comply with the Taylor Report, and with virtually no chance of expansion except upwards, the decision was made to relocate to a brand new home in 1995, with Ayresome Park being sold off to housing developers. Middlesbrough signed off in fairytale fashion, defeating Luton Town to clinch the First Division championship and gain promotion to the Premier League.

Plans for the new 30,000-seat stadium on the banks of the River Tees were given the go-ahead in the spring of 1994, and construction began that autumn, with the new Riverside Stadium being ready for the 1995–96 season. Ayresome Park was retained as a training ground for a year until the new facility was opened, and it was finally demolished in early 1997. It is now a housing estate, but road names like The Midfield and The Turnstile give some indication as to the area's former usage.

In 2005 the club installed the old Ayresome Park gates in front of the Riverside Stadium, showing appreciation for their former residence that once figured on the world stage.

After a seven-year spell in the Championship, Middlesbrough were promoted back in the Premier League in 2016. Sadly, this elevation was to last for just a single season and they were demoted again at the end of the 2016–17 season.

Ayresome Park's North Stand, 1992.

Millwall

The Den

Address: Cold Blow Lane, New Cross, London SE14

Highest attendance: 48,672 v Derby County, 20 February 1937

First league match: Millwall 2–0 v Bristol Rovers, 28 August 1920

Final league match: Millwall 0–3 v Bristol Rovers, 8 May 1993

International matches: England (1911), England 'B' (1989)

Ground layout: Main Stand, Ilderton Road End, North Bank, Cold Blow Lane End

Status: Demolished

Current stadium: The (New) Den

Right: East End Terrace, 1968.

The Den was quite simply the most intimidating ground in the Football League. From Millwall's arrival as a Southern League side in 1910 to their departure 83 years later, no team or supporter was keen to experience the frightening atmosphere and the 'Millwall roar', and the ground was shut no less than five times by the FA owing to crowd trouble, an unwanted record.

In 1910 Tom Thorne, the director in charge, had sought the help of architect Archibald Leitch and builders Humphries of Knightsbridge. The estimated cost of the Den was £10,000. A small Main Stand only was in evidence.

Millwall's first league match at the Den was on 28 August 1920. They beat Bristol Rovers 2–0. The game was played in the Football League Third Division South of which Millwall were founder members. In that year Millwall scored 83 goals at the Den. This is still a Football League record.

Being in close proximity to the Surrey commercial docks, the Den sustained severe bomb damage during the Blitz and a German bomb hit the North

The last game at the Den – the South Stand, 1993.

the ground being described as at best rudimentary or basic.

However, despite its austerity, it possessed a ferocious atmosphere. No opposition team or supporter relished a trip to this part of London. So much so that Millwall at the Den went on a two-and-a-half-year unbeaten run of 59 home games between 1964 and 1967. In 1974 the ground made history when it witnessed the very first league match to be played on a Sunday; this was a local derby against Fulham.

By the late 1970s, the Den had fallen into disrepair and there were proposals to build a 'Super-Den' on the existing sites of the Den and the adjacent disused New Cross Stadium, with an anticipated all-seater capacity of between 25,000 and 30,000. However, the club could not raise sufficient funds to pay for the ambitious and popular project and it eventually fell through.

By 1985 the club's chief executive acknowledged that the club could be forced to move to a new stadium and possibly even change its name in a desperate attempt to tackle the club's growing reputation for football hooliganism.

New owners took over in 1986, and money began to be spent on ground improvement: a new family enclosure, new crush barriers, resurfaced terraces, a television gantry, new catering booths, improved toilets, new seats in two stands, improved steps, new floodlights, new turnstiles and a new exit. Around £1 million was spent and yet despite all this the ground, to many, looked hardly any different.

Events on the pitch improved, and the stadium hosted First Division football from 1988 to 1990, but within a year of Millwall's relegation it was confirmed that the club would indeed move to a new 20,000 all-seater stadium at Senegal Fields, a quarter of a mile away from Cold Blow Lane. The new stadium was situated in a more spacious location and also allowed for the development of a sports centre for public use.

The sale of the old stadium to property developers was completed on 11 December 1991 at a cost of £6.5 million, although Millwall would continue to play

Terrace on 19 April 1943. A week later another attack caused a fire that destroyed the Main Stand. The club accepted offers from three London neighbours in order to continue to stage games. On 24 February 1944 Millwall returned to the Den. This was achieved in part with considerable volunteer labour by the Lions' fans.

After the war, rationing in Great Britain continued and Millwall were refused permission by the Ministry of Works to construct a new two-tier stand, despite having procured all the materials. They had to wait until 1948, when permission was granted to build a smaller single-tier stand two thirds the length of the pitch, with a forecourt terrace at the front. Archibald Leitch's trademark gables were never replaced.

Two sides of the ground were large areas of concrete terraces with basic crush barriers built up on earth banks, and the Ilderton Road End was similar. By the mid-1950s, however, all four sides had some form of cover, with pitched roofs covering only the rear third, meaning that fans had to congregate at the back to stay dry.

The Ilderton Road end had a concrete, brick and steel-framed stand built above the ground. The hill where the old New Cross Stadium once stood had an excellent free view into the ground and was nicknamed Jews Hill. The club put up high advertising hoardings to prevent their free entertainment. The Main Stand was small, with plenty of stanchions supporting the low-pitched roof.

On 5 October 1953 Millwall played Manchester United to mark the opening of their floodlights. A crowd of over 25,000 saw the Lions beat the Red Devils 2–1. Little changed at the Den after that with there for nearly 18 months afterwards. The move to the New Den took place in August 1993. The demolition of the old stadium commenced that autumn.

The site is now occupied by new houses and flats; however the site and surrounding area are now known to locals as 'Little Millwall' and fans still make the trip by foot from New Cross Gate station through the area to the all-seater New Den.

When Millwall moved, it was the first stadium to comply with the Taylor Report, due to its being under construction when the report was published.

It seemed as though the 'New London Stadium', as it was first named, albeit briefly, would be a wholly different place from the Den. Nearly two decades on, however, the 'New' has been dropped from the ground's name and the ground is as intimidating as ever – proving, perhaps, that you can take the Lions out of the Den but you can't take the Den out of the Lions.

In January 2017 Millwall Football Club admitted for the first time that they may be forced to leave their south London home and relocate to Kent should the seizure of their land go ahead following Lewisham Council's plan to compulsorily purchase areas around the Den.

Millwall have seen considerable cup success in the last two decades, but have experienced a rollercoaster ride in the league. However after a late surge in 2017 and finishing sixth, Millwall were promoted to the Championship from League One after winning the play-off final.

The Den's North side, 1968.

Morecambe

Christie Park

Address: Lancaster Road, Morecambe, Lancashire LA4 5TJ

Highest attendance: 9,383 v Weymouth (FA Cup), 6 January 1962

First league match: Morecambe 0-0 v Barnet, 11 August 2007

Final league match: Morecambe 2-1 v Dagenham & Redbridge, 20 May 2010

Ground-sharing: Carlisle United (temporary 2005)

Ground layout: Main Stand, North Stand, Umbro Stand, Car Wash Terrace

Status: Demolished

Current stadium: Globe Arena

Right: The North Terrace, 1995, just prior to building a covered stand.

Opposite above: The Car Wash Terrace, 1995.

Opposite below: The Main Stand, 1995.

After battling throughout their whole history, Morecambe finally delivered league football to Christie Park, albeit briefly, in 2007. It was a fitting farewell to the ground as, upon promotion to the Football League, plans were already in motion for a move to a new £12 million stadium at Westgate. Originally known as Roseberry Park, the ground was renamed by then president J. B. Christie and the name was retained owing to the impact of his financial assistance in the club's early years.

Morecambe were formed in 1920, but it would be nearly 90 years before they entered the Football League. Those early seasons proved difficult and it was not until 1924–25 that the club began to enjoy some success, claiming the Lancashire Combination title for the first time. This was later followed by success in the Lancashire Junior Cup, beating old rivals Chorley after two replays. Christie handed the ownership to Morecambe Council in 1927 shortly before his death, securing the immediate future of both club and stadium. The handover condition was that if Morecambe ever folded, the site should be used as a playground for the town's children.

The ground was originally designed to be an oval shape similar to that of Lancaster City's ground at Giant Axe with stands on all four sides. The plans were altered, however, and the ground constructed in a normal fashion with a wooden stand built to hold 700 that lasted until the Main Stand was built in 1962.

For 30 years it was a struggle until Ken Horton was appointed player-manager in 1956 and this saw a visible and marked improvement both on the field and off it. The Auxiliary Supporters' Club was then formed and with their help, many ground improvements were undertaken, with the next major improvement being the building of banking on the Lancaster Road side of the pitch using tons of cinders.

With crowds rising, the town end (North Stand) was concreted and a roofed standing area built. This was opened on 27 September 1958. The club's first major floodlights were erected as well and opened officially on 27 October 1960 when an All Star XI lost 3–4 to a Morecambe side. In a period of great change, the

92

new £10,000 Auxiliary Club was opened just a few weeks later on 7 December 1960.

6 January 1962 saw Christie Park draw its biggest ever crowd when officially 9,383 paid to watch Morecambe's FA Cup third-round tie against Weymouth. At the end of that 1961–62 season, the Main Stand with 500 seats was built at a cost of £20,000. The stand sat on the halfway line, covered roughly half the pitch and had terracing in front of it.

In all, the club spent more than £35,000 in the space of a few months on ground improvements, a figure that would be around £1 million today. The new stand was officially opened on 17 October 1962 by the club chairman after a commemorative friendly with Leeds United.

There was a covered area, known as the 'Scratching Shed', at the Lancaster Road (South Stand) end of the ground, and with a number of repairs down the years it lasted until 1968. Then another major step in the shaping of the modern Christie Park saw the stand demolished and a new £8,000 covered terrace built; this was named the Umbro Stand.

In 1974 the club won the FA Trophy at Wembley. Difficult times for the club followed, until a brighter picture emerged in the mid-1980s, but the club had to work on improvements in all areas to achieve its next step up.

It was 25 years before the ground was altered again when new floodlights, costing £40,000, were erected in 1993 and officially opened by the great Sir Tom Finney on 4 August prior to a friendly with Burnley. This was the start of a major facelift for the ground as the club endeavoured to prepare for Conference football. Grass bankings were replaced by concrete terracing and with a general tidy up the Shrimps were ready to move up the pyramid when that opportunity arose in 1995.

The terracing opposite the Main Stand remained uncovered throughout and was known as the Car Wash Terrace owing to the vehicle cleaning service situated behind it.

The ground work didn't stop on elevation, and the club took the ambitious step of building a new £560,000 North Stand at the town end of the ground. The stand was first used by supporters on Saturday 21 March 1997 in a Conference fixture with Cheltenham Town but officially opened by Sir Bobby Charlton on 2 September prior to a friendly with a full-strength Southampton side.

The club enjoyed successful spells in the Conference for a decade, and the greatest moment in the club's history came in 2006 when they achieved promotion to the Football League, beating Exeter City 2–1 in the play-off final at Wembley.

Following this promotion, the club announced plans to move to a new ground in the Westgate area. Despite the new stand, much of Christie Park was seemingly unfit for purpose, although strangely plans were in place and approved for a new £1 million three-tier stand.

The 2009–10 season was to be Morecambe's last at Christie Park, the club's home for 89 years. They surpassed every pundit's predictions to finish fourth, earning the chance to participate in the League Two play-offs. However, they lost 2–7 on aggregate to Dagenham and Redbridge. A 0–6 away battering rendered the second leg almost meaningless, but Sammy McIlroy encouraged his team to a 2–1 win in the last-ever game at Christie Park. The gates of the ground were closed for the last time on the evening of Sunday 23 May by Morecambe Chief Executive Rod Taylor.

The Shrimps then moved on to their first season at the Globe Arena, the new stadium named after the construction company that built it. Christie Park would sadly not have the idealistic use that its former owner envisaged. The council over-ruled the benefactor's wishes, using the cash to allegedly fund the new stadium.

Within days of the end of the 2009–10 season, demolition of the stadium commenced and site clearance began. By mid-August 2010 the superstructure of a new supermarket occupied the

spot where the stadium once stood, and it opened around three months later. The 6,400-capacity stadium's relationship with league football was all too brief, and its name was a reminder of the man who kick-started Morecambe's journey to get there.

Despite not pulling up any trees, Morecambe continue to consolidate and remain steadily placed in League Two.

Newport County

Somerton Park

Address: Cromwell Road, Newport, Gwent NP19 0GD

Highest attendance: 24,268 v Cardiff City, 16 October 1937

First league match: Newport County 0–1 v Reading, 28 August 1920

Final league match: Newport County 0–1 v Rochdale, 7 May 1988

Other usages: Greyhound Racing, Speedway

Ground layout: Main Stand, Social Club/Popular Side, Cromwell Road End, Railway End

Status: Demolished

Current stadium: Rodney Parade

Somerton Park was the site of Newport County's greatest years but also their worst – the period leading up to their demise in 1989. Throughout most of their tenure they were marginalised by their other tenants, both common stadium-sharers in the past in Britain; firstly the Cardiff Arms Park Greyhound Racing Company and, latterly, Newport Wasps speedway team. The club purchased the ground outright in 1980 but only enjoyed it for nine years before they dropped out of the Football League and folded.

In April 1912 Newport County had been accepted to play in the Second Division of the Southern League for the 1912–13 season. Shortly afterwards the site for the ground which formed part of the old Somerton estate was obtained by the club's chairman, Bert Moss. Hundreds of loads of rubbish and earth were tipped and banked around a pitch. The only covered accommodation consisted of a wooden hut at the side and that was reserved for the press.

The newly acquired premises at Somerton Park remained Newport County's home during their league days. The stadium was almost sold for housing in June 1919, but it was rescued, purchased and transferred to a committee of employees from the John Lysaght's steel works. Newport then joined the Football League for the 1919–20 season at the expense of Stalybridge Celtic.

The Social Club/Popular Side was originally the main stand at Somerton Park. It dates back to the 1920s. The Main Stand was built in the 1930s and originally had terracing at its front. Latterly this side of the ground comprised two separate covered stands, one with seating, and one with terracing.

Behind the goals were the Cromwell Road End and the Railway End. The former was a covered terrace with bench seats and the latter nothing more than an open, shallow gravel bank from which to watch the game. Not much was done to the ground in its entire history, the main modifications occurring to accommodate Somerton's other sports.

The two Main Stands, 1981.

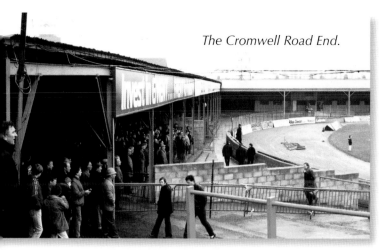

The Cromwell Road End.

On 17 November 1932 the first greyhound meeting took place at the stadium, and the pitch was moved to fit the dog-racing track. The venue was popular and formed a close relationship with the football team for over 30 years with meetings every Tuesday and Friday. Newport County and Somerton Park saw Second Division football just prior to the outbreak of the Second World War, a period which included their record attendance against arch-rivals Cardiff City.

Greyhound racing began to experience lower attendances and by 1963 the decision was taken to close the track. The stadium was then home to the Newport Wasps speedway team between 1964 and 1977, attracting some the biggest names in the sport. The tight track meant that turf had to be brought on to make the corner flag area for football matches and removed once the match had finished.

The early 1980s were also a time of success for Newport, narrowly missing a return to the Second Division and witnessing European football at the stadium through winning the Welsh Cup in 1980.

These were to be the precursor to tragedy, however, as County suffered successive relegations to drop out of the Football League, and the club sold Somerton Park back to the local council to clear some of their debts.

The club were wound up a year later on 27 February 1989 with debts of £330,000 after failing to complete their Conference fixtures. Their bankruptcy saw them expelled from that league. The club was re-formed as Newport AFC within four months and began the 1989–90 season as an Hellenic League side.

The new club's first season was spent in Moreton-in-Marsh around 80 miles north-east of Newport, as Newport Council had considered the new company to be a continuation of the old and had thus refused them permission to use Somerton Park on the grounds of unpaid rent.

The team immediately won the Hellenic double, winning promotion to the Southern League. The ground was then reopened for two seasons for the newly-formed club to play there until the 1992–93 season, but the club was then cruelly moved on again. Newport were exiled to England for a further two seasons, ground-sharing with Gloucester City.

The club was also forced to resort to legal action to protect themselves from being forced out of the English Football League system. That litigation proved successful, a landmark High Court verdict enabling them to have a permanent home in Newport at the then newly-built Newport Stadium. The stadium though was like the Withdean Stadium, an athletics arena with a football pitch in the middle.

Somerton Park was demolished in 1993 to make way for housing, and from housing three sports clubs to housing families it was now another ground reduced to mere memories. At least the new development continued to bear the ground's name.

In 1999 the club reverted to the name Newport County AFC and in 2010 they were promoted to the Conference Premier. In 2012, after 18 years at the Newport Stadium, they moved to Rodney Parade, ground-sharing with Newport Gwent Dragons Rugby Club. In 2013 the club were promoted back to the Football League after an absence of 25 years.

Newport Stadium - see page 157.

The Popular Side and Cromwell Road End, 1995.

Address: Abington Avenue, Northampton NN1 4PR

Highest attendance: 24,523 v Fulham, 23 April 1966

First league match: Northampton Town 4–1 v Grimsby, 4 September 1920

Final league match: Northampton Town 0–1 v Mansfield Town, 11 October 1994

Other usages: Cricket

Ground layout: Main Stand, Hotel End, Spion Kop, Cricket Side

Status: Extant

Current stadium: Sixfields Stadium

Before moving to the new Sixfields Stadium in 1994, Northampton Town had previously had only one home ground, the County Ground. The Club, nicknamed the Cobblers after the town's long association with the shoe industry, had played at the site since their formation in 1897 and their admittance to the Midland League the year after. They were elected to the Football League in 1920. They shared the venue and were probably the poor relations of Northamptonshire County Cricket Club.

A small Main Stand had been constructed prior to the First World War with terracing to either side. In 1924 a new Main Stand was constructed that ran the full length of the pitch, with a players' tunnel underneath, the club raising £5,000 to support this. There were also improvements made to terracing in the Hotel End.

Sadly, this Main Stand facility was almost completely destroyed by fire in December 1929 and had to be rebuilt, the damage estimated at around £5,000. The source of the fire was thought to be in the away dressing room. However this rebuild was completed by August 1930. This covered stand had seating to the rear and terracing to the front.

The majority of home supporters congregated in the Hotel End, a terrace behind one of the goals. This end was covered after the Second World War. Opposite was the Spion Kop, a deceptively titled uncovered terrace, much smaller than its name suggested. It remained uncovered for the entire life of the ground.

Completing the layout was what was known as the Cricket Side. The ground was unusual in the respect that it was situated on the edge of the cricket ground. The club shared the site with Northamptonshire

Right: The open Kop End, 1966.

Below: The Hotel End, 1988.

CCC. This meant that one side of the ground was completely open. For popular games, such as FA Cup ties, temporary seating was erected along this open side, but normally this comprised just a series of wooden planks laid on the ground, around three to four people in depth.

The football pitch gained the reputation of having the worst playing surface in the league, which was largely the result of the pitch being used as a spectator area, car park and picnic area during the cricket season.

Floodlights were installed at the County ground in October 1960. The 1960s period was remarkable for the Cobblers as between 1958 and 1965 under Dave Bowen they rose all the way from the Fourth Division to the First. However, by 1970 they were back in the Fourth.

The Main Stand was re-roofed in 1980, and new floodlights were installed at the beginning of the 1980–81 season. However, when they were first used, for a match against Southend United, they failed, and the match had to be abandoned!

The Main Stand survived until 1985, but following the Bradford disaster, it was deemed to be unsafe and was then demolished, leaving only the terracing remaining. A small temporary Main Stand was erected in 1986, which sat astride the halfway line and was mockingly nicknamed the 'Meccano Stand' by fans, owing to its resemblance to the model construction kit.

From the 1970s to the 1990s the team occupied the Third and Fourth Divisions, with the team finishing rock bottom of the league in 1994. However, they kept their place as the stadium of Kidderminster Harriers, the Football Conference winners, did not meet the standard required for promotion.

By this stage, however, construction work on the new 7,600 all-seater Sixfields Stadium had started. The new stadium was still under construction when the 1994–95 season began, and so the club started that season still at the County Ground. The Cobblers

played their last game there on 12 October 1994, and then moved to Sixfields, a four-sided stadium more suitable for football.

The County Ground remains in situ, solely used for cricket now, the only reminder of football days being the Hotel End turnstiles, which still form part of the perimeter of the County Ground land. An indoor cricket school now lies on the site of the football pitch.

After a turbulent few years, the Cobblers took the Division Two title in 2015–16, and currently play in League One.

The replacement Main Stand, 1988.

The old Main Stand.

Address: London Road, Headington, Oxford
OX3 7RS

Highest attendance: 22,730 v Preston
North End (FA Cup), 29 February 1964

First league match: Oxford United 2–1
v Lincoln City, 22 August 1962

Final league match: Oxford United 1–1
v Port Vale, 1 May 2001

Ground layout: Beech Road Stand/Main
Stand, Osler Road Stand, London Road End,
Cuckoo Lane End

Status: Demolished

Current stadium: Kassam Stadium

Below: The London Road Stand, 1973.

Opposite top: Osler Road Stand, 1969.

For nearly half its history, the Manor Ground was home to Headington United, who became Oxford United in 1960, shortly before heading into the Football League in 1962, replacing Accrington Stanley. United had moved to the Manor Ground from Britannia Field in 1925 with the city's cricket, tennis and bowls clubs. Twenty-five years later, football was the only sport being played at the stadium.

The first stand to be built was the Manor Club, nestled in the corner between where the Main Stand and the uncovered northerly sloping terracing of the Cuckoo Lane End would later be.

Only a handful of Football League clubs had installed floodlights when Headington United proudly used theirs for the first time in December 1950 with a friendly against local side Banbury Spencer. These were borrowed and put up on 36 wooden poles.

By 1953 the side won the first of its Southern League championships and in 1954 reached the fourth round of the FA Cup beating league clubs Millwall and Stockport County on the way before losing 2–4 to Bolton Wanderers. They promptly purchased the ground from the council for £10,000.

Ambitious ground improvements were then undertaken at The Manor, with one of the most modern seated stands in the land for that era, The Beech Road Stand (Main Stand), being erected in the west in 1957, in anticipation of the day when league football would be seen at the ground. This stand came courtesy of a gift of £33,000 from the supporters' club. Permanent floodlights were also installed at the same time.

Home terracing was the London Road Stand to the south, again constructed with the assistance of supporters' club funds; the Osler Road Stand was to the east and the Cuckoo Lane End to the north. The ground changed little in its lifetime.

As late as 1959 Headington United became full-time professionals, and the next year they changed their name to Oxford United. At the time, this was a very unpopular move with the people of Headington who considered that they weren't Oxford and that the neighbouring community had done little to get the club or the team to their current standing.

In 1961 Headington Sports Ground Ltd sold the football ground to Oxford United for £8,800. The price was low, probably because the land was safeguarded by a restrictive covenant as to its use. League football duly arrived in 1962 at the expense of the defunct Accrington Stanley, and six years later Oxford found themselves competing at the giddy heights of the Second Division. Some of this success may have been down to the small, awkward pitch which sloped from end to end and from corner to corner.

1964 saw the record attendance at the ground when almost 23,000 crammed in for an FA Cup tie with Preston North End. Oxford, at that time,

became the first-ever Fourth Division side to reach the quarter-finals.

In 1966, with the demolition of Sandfield College, a new entrance to the ground was created onto London Road. In reality the ground was then seven stands, being described as 'the strangest collection of constructions ever assembled around a football pitch'.

The Beech Road Stand was covered and seated although it ran only halfway along the side of the pitch. The London Road End was simple terracing with a corrugated iron roof along the full length. The Osler Road side was actually three covered terrace stands, each one reducing in height, the lowest being described as looking like a bike shed. Some of this was standing and some seated.

The Cuckoo Lane End was an open and exposed terrace, primarily for away fans. The layout was completed by the original north-west corner Manor Club, which consisted of two very small stands for players' friends and families.

United enjoyed perhaps their best success at the Manor Ground in the 1980s as they competed in the First Division and even won the League Cup in 1986, the prospect of European football thwarted by the ban on English clubs after the Heysel disaster.

Robert Maxwell took over Oxford United in 1981 but failed in his attempt to merge it with Reading to form Thames Valley Royals in 1983. On his death in 1991 the club passed into the hands of the receivers, who sold it the next year to Biomass Recycling Ltd.

By this time, with sterner safety regulations being imposed on football grounds in Britain, the poorly-maintained Manor Ground was crumbling and becoming increasingly outdated. Redeveloping the ground had been judged as far too costly and the location was extremely restricted, being hemmed in by suburban semis, a hospital and a bowls club. Although more seats were forced in where possible, it became clear a move would soon be on the cards.

Biomass Recycling sold the club to motor-racer Robin Herd in 1995 and in that same year Oxford City

Council granted the club permission to build a new purpose-built all-seater stadium at Minchery Farm on the outskirts of the city, and work started the next year, but then came to a two-year halt through lack of funds.

Construction of the new stadium resumed in 1999 following a takeover deal by millionaire Firoz Kassam who purchased Herd's shares and set about clearing the club's debts. Oxford finally moved to the Kassam Stadium in 2001.

The last league match at the Manor was on 1 May 2001 when Oxford drew 1–1 with Port Vale. Oxford's final season at the Manor Ground was one of the worst in their history. They finished bottom of Division Two with a mere 27 points and were relegated to Division Three, their lowest standing in 35 years.

The Manor Ground was demolished almost immediately and on the site were built some flats and a hospital named The Manor Hospital which replaced the Acland Hospital on the Banbury Road – a pleasant change from the popular option of a retail park.

Oxford United would experience mixed fortunes at their new home. Having said goodbye to the Manor

they dropped out of the Football League five years later in 2006, only to return via the Conference play-offs in 2010. Changes of ownership and managers led to an uncertain five years, but in 2015–16 they began to lift themselves back towards happier times with promotion to League One.

The Cuckoo Lane End, 1988.

Port Vale

The Old Recreation Ground

The Old Recreation Ground was an example of the importance of a club owning its own stadium. Port Vale moved there in 1913 and rented it from the council. It was their sixth home since their formation in 1876, having played on various fields in the area including waste ground. It was here Port Vale would adopt their club colours of black and white and achieve some of their biggest success.

Burslem Port Vale were founder members of the Second Division in 1892, before failing re-election in 1896. They returned two years later before resigning from the Football League in 1907. In 1913 Port Vale gained permission from Stoke-on-Trent Council to develop the Kent Street Recreation Ground in Hanley. The new ground was renamed the Old Recreation Ground and had room for 30,000 fans. Players had to change in converted stables with one stove and walk between houses to enter the ground until the Swan Passage Stand was built for £12,000.

Fans used to climb the nearby church ramparts by the Swan Passage side of the ground for a better view of big games, which was free, but decidedly risky. On the opposite side of the ground was the Bryan Street paddock, which was built below the level of the pitch. Most fans' heads were only just above pitch level, and on more than one occasion players would land on top of them when chasing a ball by the touchline. The two ends of the ground were called the Town End and the Clock End.

Vale's first Second Division league game at the stadium was in October 1919 after a successful third attempt at league football. They replaced the disgraced Leeds City after that club was ejected from the Football League for making illegal payments. Port Vale took over the remaining fixtures.

By 1927 Vale were concerned with the stadium's lack of space and a move back to a re-vamped previous ground, the 50,000 capacity Cobridge Stadium, was suggested. However, after problems with the council, the plan collapsed. Vale's response, after a period of stability in the league, was to purchase their ground. The Valiants then went on to achieve their highest ever league position, fifth in the Second Division, in 1931, something they have yet to equal at their current home.

Eventually mounting debts, primarily £3,000 in loans to the club's late president, saw them sell their prized asset back to the council 16 years later for £13,500, a move that would take the club's future out of their own hands. The council initially refused to allow the club to play at their ground at all, but eventually relented for a rent of £400 a year on a short-term lease.

The stadium was in a rather bad condition anyway, especially following years of neglect during the Second World War. The dressing rooms were bare, there were no toilet facilities throughout the entire ground, and racing pigeons were kept by the local paper and a number of supporters so as to relay the scoreline to different parts of the city.

Port Vale's remaining stay at The Old Recreation Ground was then all too brief, as the city council decided to construct a giant indoor shopping centre on the land, forcing them to look elsewhere.

Grand plans were drawn up for the 'Wembley of the North', but the new stadium at Vale Park fell way short of this lofty advertisement owing to the club's financial position and the lack of material following the Second World War. The club were fast running out of money and unable to complete the ambitious new stands it intended. The ground would simply be windswept banks of terracing without any cover for fans unless a cheaper solution could be found.

As a last resort, the club asked if it could remove the Swan Passage Stand from the Old Recreation Ground and re-erect it at Vale Park. The application was initially rejected, but eventually the council relented. Vale Park had its first covered stand until the Railway Stand was built some years later.

Later, when the new Bycars Stand was erected at Vale Park, the old Swan Passage was nearly all demolished except for a small portion that was kept intact above the 'family stand' corner. That remains the roof of the stand to this day. That small stand is now well over a hundred years old making it by some distance the oldest structure at Vale Park and it is also the only part of the Old Recreation Ground that is still in existence.

On the site of Vale's old home now stands the multi-storey car park for the Potteries Shopping Centre. The stadium is now of a different generation of Vale fans, but it was the site where the foundations were laid for the club's history.

Turbulent times including administration have hindered Port Vale and poor form in 2017 saw them relegated from League One by just one point.

Right: Aerial view - Aerofilms

Reading

Address: Norfolk Road, Reading, Berkshire RG3 2EF

Highest attendance: 33,042 v Brentford (FA Cup), 19 February 1927

First league match: Reading 1-2 v Gillingham, 1 September 1920

Final league match: Reading 0-1 v Norwich, 3 May 1998

Ground layout: North Stand/Norfolk Road, South Stand/Tilehurst Terrace/South Bank, West Stand/Tilehurst End, East Stand/Reading End/Town End

Status: Demolished

Current stadium: Madejski Stadium

Right: Norfolk Road Stand, 1970.

Opposite top: Tilehurst Terrace, 1989.

Opposite bottom: Town End, 1997.

When Reading moved to Elm Park in 1896 they had already been in existence for 25 years, unusual for a team in the South. They had spells at the Reading Recreation Ground and Reading Cricket Ground, then latterly Coley Park and Caversham Cricket Ground. Elm Park, built on an old gravel pit and into a hill, was to be Reading's first league home, however, when they were elected to the Third Division in 1920. Prior to this they had been founder members of the Southern League in 1894, turning professional a year later.

A possible move to another site arose in 1908, when the club's annual general meeting proposed moving to a new ground near Reading railway station. A board meeting the following year decided that the move would not be possible, due to the 'actions of the GWR' (Great Western Railway).

The stadium remained largely unchanged for the duration of its existence. Upon Reading's arrival, there was already cover on half the Norfolk Road Stand, this wrapping round to cover half the Town End; however, it was short-lived as it fell victim to a gale. It was swiftly replaced by an all-wooden main

stand that could seat 4,000 and would remain in place until the club left; this covered terrace running the length of the Norfolk Road side of the pitch, with upholstered seats later installed, would be the only stand in the stadium that allowed spectators to sit.

During the Second World War, an enemy bomb destroyed the club's offices, but these were in the town centre and the ground survived. After the war, shelter was erected on the opposite Tilehurst Terrace covering the centre section, with a clock adorning the centre. The flanks quickly followed at the turn of the 1950s; these were at a different height to the original section. This stand provided cover for 6,000.

Floodlights were installed and used for the first time in a match with Carlisle on 27 February 1956. They were upgraded three years later. Behind the goals were the uncovered Tilehurst End for the home fans and the Town End for the visitors; these terraces remained open for the ground's lifetime.

As a result of Reading's relegation to the Fourth Division after the 1982–83 season, the club was threatened with a merger with Oxford United, a move which would have seen the closure of Elm Park and the formation of the Thames Valley Royals. The announcement from Robert Maxwell on 16 April 1983 came from nowhere, without any prior hints or tip-offs. Such a furore ensued from the two separate communities that Maxwell's plans were eventually dropped.

£160,000 was spent on safety work in the mid-1980s and some of the seats in the stand would no longer stay upright due to slight subsidence.

After challenging in the First Division in the 1990s, and now bound by the Taylor Report, the club believed that the Premier League was attainable, so converting the rusting and poorly maintained Elm Park into an all-seater stadium would have been totally impractical.

The club moved to a new stadium in time for the 1998–99 season, with Elm Park succumbing to housing. The new development retains the ground's

name. The 24,000-capacity Madejski Stadium, named after chairman John Madejski, was primed for top-flight football, but unfortunately the Royals' last season at Elm Park resulted in relegation to the Second Division, and it would be eight years before they reached the promised land.

Since that time, the Royals have enjoyed a second spell in the Premier League and at the end of the 2016–17 season were denied a third term by a narrow loss on penalties in the play-off final.

Rotherham United

Address: Millmoor Lane, Rotherham, Yorkshire S60 1HR

Highest attendance: 25,170 v Sheffield United, 13 December 1952

First league match: Rotherham County 2-0 v Nottingham Forest, 30 August 1919

Final league match: Rotherham United 1-0 v Barnet, 3 May 2008

Other usages: Greyhound Racing (1931-1933)

Ground layout: Main Stand, Millmoor Lane Stand, Tivoli End, Railway End

Status: Extant

Current stadium: New York Stadium (AESSEAL New York Stadium)

Right: The Millmoor Lane Stand, April 1970.

Opposite above: The Main Stand in the 1970s.

Opposite below: Tivoli End, 1991.

The result of a merger between neighbouring Rotherham Town and Rotherham County, United played at the latter's home of Millmoor after uniting in 1925, and assumed County's Football League position and fixtures. Far from idyllic, Millmoor was built and opened in 1907 on the site of a flour mill, later surrounded by scrapyards and a dilapidated cinema, and as such made for a cramped environment, with everyone residing and working on top of one another. There is a suggestion that the ground was so named because it was surrounded by mills and moors.

Two small stands were brought from their previous home at the Red House ground, while the ground's steep slopes was lessened as much as possible by a team of hard-working volunteers.

Millmoor remained fairly basic until County were elected to the Second Division in 1919 and a year later built the core of what was then the first Main Stand. However, times remained tough, and United struggled to build a modest 40yd roof on the Millmoor Lane side. The building structure followed American practice and was the first of its type in Britain. At either end behind the goals were the uncovered Railway End terrace and the Tivoli End terrace, the latter named after the rustic cinema situated behind it.

Rotherham tried to ease their financial matters by starting greyhound racing in 1931. But two years later they were ordered to cease forthwith by the Football League. In 1949 United finally managed to buy Millmoor from the railway company, and over the next few years set about concreting the terraces and expanding the Tivoli End in 1951. The Railway End was the first to be improved, covered in 1957.

The 1960s saw four changes. Floodlights were erected in 1960 and in 1964 the Main Stand roof was

extended with a lower roof to cover the paddock. A year later a gym was built alongside the stand and finally in 1968 the Tivoli End was roofed.

During the 1970s seating was added under the Millmoor Lane Stand roof, followed by more seats under a new roof added next to the old one in 1982. In 1987 the club was bought by Ken Booth, owner of the scrapyard which surrounded Millmoor on three sides of the ground.

The Tivoli End was the end for the home fans and could hold up to 2,700. It was later seated during the club's time in the Football League Championship.

The Railway End was where up to 2,000 away fans could be accommodated. The railway referred to in the stand's name was the now closed line to the former Rotherham Westgate railway station. Again this was a former basic terrace with seats added later.

The Millmoor Lane Stand ended as a mismatch of three stands. Near the Tivoli End was the small, uncovered area of seating, which ran for a third of the length of the pitch. Next to that was the oldest, all-seated stand with sloping roof with many pillars, which again ran for about a third of the pitch, but this time straddling the halfway line. The third, and comparatively modern looking part, had a seating area slightly bigger than the other two parts of the stand, and possessed a roof that didn't slope, but still contained a few supporting stilt pillars.

Towards the end of Rotherham's time at Millmoor the facilities were deemed sub-standard for both supporters and opposing teams, with West Ham players refusing to change in the Millmoor dressing rooms in 2001. The lack of comfort proved to be to Rotherham's advantage that day, as they defeated the Hammers.

Things quickly took a turn for the worse for both United and Millmoor, as the team suffered two relegations and fell from the second tier to the basement in just three seasons. Severe financial difficulties, administration and subsequent points deductions helped accelerate the process. There were many changes at board level, but events never seemed to quite resolve themselves.

Despite all this, work commenced on a brand new Main Stand in 2006. Further trouble was brewing, however, and the club could not agree a new lease with the ground owners, resulting in a very public and acrimonious fall-out. All work on the new stand ceased, with the club refusing to put any more money into the stand or give any commitment to modernising the ground until a rental and other conditions could be agreed. These were not forthcoming and almost a decade later, the skeletal stand remains unfinished.

The Millers spent the majority of the 2007–08 season in the automatic promotion places but in mid-March 2008 it was revealed that Rotherham had again entered administration and would be deducted 10 points. Local businessman Tony Stewart then took over as chairman for the 2008–09 season and took the club out of administration via a CVA agreement, resulting in a 17-point deduction.

Feeling that their options were now exhausted, the club then decided to exile themselves and move temporarily to the Don Valley Stadium in Sheffield, ground-sharing with Sheffield Eagles Rugby League club and City of Sheffield Athletics Club; this would continue until they could complete a new stadium in Rotherham.

In May 2011 Rotherham Titans and Rotherham Council announced a plan to allow the rugby union club to move into Millmoor, but withdrew the scheme six months after the deal fell through.

The new purpose-built community facility The New York Stadium back in Rotherham was started in June 2011 and the stadium was officially opened by Prince Edward, Duke of Kent, on 12 March 2012. The 12,000 capacity stadium cost around £20 million to build. It is United's new home. Meanwhile, the decaying corpse of Millmoor still sits appropriately amongst the scrapyards, used only for occasional non-league or Sunday matches.

Despite being settled in a new home, instability has continued on the field with the club yo-yoing between the Championship and League One.

Don Valley Stadium - see page 158.

Rushden & Diamonds

Nene Park

Address: Nene Park, Irthlingborough, Northants NN9 5QF

Highest attendance: 6,431 v Leeds United (FA Cup), 2 January 1999

First league match: Rushden & Diamonds 0–0 v Lincoln City, 16 August 2001

Final league match: Rushden & Diamonds 1–2 v Barnet, 6 May 2006

International matches: England U-21, England C

Ground layout: North Stand, South Stand, West Stand/Peter DeBanke Terrace, East Stand/Airwair Stand

Status: Extant

Current stadium: Not applicable – club wound up

Right: Peter DeBanke Terrace, 1997.

Despite the bland name for a particularly adventurously titled club, Nene Park is rather idyllically situated on the banks of the River Nene. The stadium, constructed in 1969, pre-dates its incumbents whose formation in 1992 was the result of a merger between Rushden Town and Irthlingborough Diamonds, who were both struggling at the time. The stadium had been acquired by the Irthlingborough Diamonds from the water board many years before the union. Nene Park was chosen because Rushden Town's stadium at Hayden Road was not considered up to the standard required.

In 1978 Nene Park became the first United Counties League stadium to have floodlights; they were turned on by Sir Bobby Robson.

The whole stadium was systematically redeveloped very soon after the merger at an estimated cost of £30 million, beginning in 1993 with the all-seater North Stand. When completed it could seat 1,000 spectators. The opposite South Stand quickly followed in 1994, the original stand being demolished and replaced by one very similar to the North Stand to complete the flanking of the pitch.

In addition, the newly-built Diamond Centre housed everything from the players' and staff dressing rooms to conference rooms, and a restaurant was opened. The ground, complete with a newly-laid

pitch and new floodlights, was looking ready for league football. The new structures were officially opened in April 1995 by HRH the Prince of Wales.

The Peter DeBanke Terrace, named in memory of a former player and respected servant of both clubs, was next to be completed behind the west goal, a simple covered terrace sheltering 1,800 standing spectators that was nevertheless in keeping with its all-seated neighbours.

Behind the opposite goal on the east side would be the focal point of the new Nene Park, the seated Airwair Stand completed in 1997. Initially roofless in order to be completed and eligible for league status, the arched roof added later would be the highlight of the stadium, which took the capacity to nearly 6,500. The original plans also included the addition of a second tier should the club reach the Football League; however, this was never added.

Finally, the new North Stand underwent some further significant improvements. The press box was relocated further east along the stand to make room for brand new corporate boxes at the back of the structure. Behind the stand, new offices and administration facilities were built, as well as a 150-square-metre-club shop. The new complex was opened in July 1998 by the club chairman. Equipped with the most modern ground in non-league football, it was no surprise when Nene Park eventually hosted league competition in 2001 just nine years after forming, possibly a record in modern times.

After reaching the play-offs in their first season in Nationwide Division Three, Rushden & Diamonds won the division title the following year, only to be relegated back to the lowest division in 2004. In 2005 the chairman and family (Max Griggs of Doc Martens) decided to sever their connections and offered to give the club to the newly formed Supporters' Trust. The 2005–06 season proved disastrous, as they finished last in League Two and were relegated back to the Conference.

Without the financial support of the former

chairman's family, the club struggled and in May 2011 they were fined £2,000 and docked five points for breaching the Conference's strict rules on financial management. Attempts to find a buyer came to nothing and the following month they faced a winding up order in the High Court over £750,000 in unpaid tax.

Days before the hearing, the club was expelled from the Conference whose board issued a statement that they had 'no confidence in the club's ability to pay its creditors or meet its obligations in the forthcoming season.' The club was formally wound up shortly afterwards.

Nene Park then became Kettering Town's home for 18 months, but they departed in November 2012 to play at Corby owing to the costs of running the ground. Financial issues almost led to Kettering suffering the same fate as Rushden. The stadium's biggest stand, the Airwair Stand, was closed, as falling attendances meant that keeping the stand open had become uneconomic.

In December 2012 it was reported that Coventry City were considering moving to Nene Park due to a rent dispute with their current landlords at the Ricoh Arena. However, that move did not occur as

the Sky Blues began sharing with Northampton Town. The ground and its 800-vehicle car park were left vacant with nature slowly reclaiming the site, with little immediate chance of further football use in the foreseeable future.

In September 2014 developers announced initial plans to demolish Nene Park in order to make way for a leisure park, consisting of a multi-use football facility along with entertainment and retail zones, but the plans were withdrawn six months later. Alternative plans, including community ideas, were put forward, but in January 2017 a plan was submitted to the council to demolish the stadium citing the fact that it was in a dangerous condition and represented a major fire risk.

A phoenix AFC Rushden & Diamonds was formed in 2011 as a Community Benefit Society, whose rules are registered with the FCA. The club is run by volunteers with the aim of supporting local footballers, fans and the community. The club has progressed to the eighth tier, competing in the Northern Premier League Division One South reaching the play-offs in 2016–17, and currently ground-share with Wellingborough.

Name: Athletic Ground (McCain Stadium)

Address: Seamer Road, Scarborough, North Yorkshire YO12 4HF

Highest attendance: 11,162 v Luton Town (FA Cup), 8 January 1938

First league match: Scarborough 2-2 v Wolverhampton Wanderers, 15 August 1987

Final league match: Scarborough 1-1 v Peterborough United, 8 May 1999

Ground layout: Main Stand, The Shed, East Stand, West Stand

Status: Demolished

Current stadium: Not applicable – club wound up

Scarborough FC's demise was intertwined with its home of 109 years. An old covenant preventing the site of the McCain Stadium from being used for anything other than sporting activities ultimately ended the club's dreams of selling it to pay off their debts and secure a new stadium elsewhere. The result was Scarborough being wound up in the courts in 2007.

The club arrived in 1898 after leaving the ground they shared with the cricket club; their new home was the Athletics Ground. In 1927 the Yorkshire club became professional and joined the Midland League. After only three years they became champions, breaking the record for most points in a season. The same year the club performed respectably in the FA Cup, reaching the third round before going out 1–2 to Grimsby Town who were in the nation's top league at the time.

Due to their decent performance in the Midlands League, the club were entitled to become one of the founding clubs in the new Northern Premier League in 1968. The 1970s would prove to be a successful time for the club; Scarborough FC won the FA Trophy three times at Wembley.

After several seasons consistently finishing in mid-table, the club gained a new manager in Neil Warnock, and his team became champions of the Conference in 1987. They were automatically promoted to the Football League, the first club to get there by this route.

Following this elevation, a naming-rights sponsorship deal with food giants McCain in 1988 changed the stadium name, and instead of being ashamed of the deal, indicative of the modern game, fans embraced it, ironically naming their home the 'Theatre of Chips'.

The ground had four main stands. The original Main Stand was a raised wooden construction with facilities underneath, which held about 500 bench seats. The replacement Main Stand ran along one side of the pitch. It was an old grandstand-style stand and was an all seated affair. This straddled the halfway line and had open terracing to one side.

The Shed, also known as The Cowshed, ran along the other side of the pitch and was covered terracing. This was the most popular part of the ground and was usually where the home supporters congregated. This too was centred around the halfway line with open terracing each side.

Originally both ends were open terracing. The new East Stand was behind one of the goals and was an all-seater stand in which the seats were red and the letters 'SFC' were spelled out in white seats; this opened in 1993. This was the newest part of the ground along with the West Stand, which opened two years later and was identical to the East Stand but behind the other

goal. It was where the away fans were located. Each of these stands could accommodate around 1,400 seats. The ends in the past were often referred to as the Edgehill Road End and the Seamer Road End.

In three of the four corners of the ground was uncovered terracing, although the north-west corner had become overrun with grass and weeds and so was not normally used. The other corner of the ground was two-step terracing in front of the social club known as the McCain Lounge, and included a club shop which was located in a hut. There was also a programme shop, food outlet and coffee hut.

Scarborough's introduction to the Football League in 1987 was a torrid one, as visiting Wolves fans clambered onto the corrugated roof of the away end and jumped up and down buckling all the steelwork and forcing its demolition after the game.

The club had mixed fortunes during their stay in the Football League. They spent several seasons near the bottom, but reached the play-offs for promotion twice. In May 1999 Scarborough and the McCain Stadium lost Football League status. While everyone remembers on-loan goalkeeper Jimmy Glass's goal in the final minute that kept Carlisle in the league, many forget the scenes at the McCain: hundreds of Scarborough fans already on the pitch in premature celebration of their own survival forced to sit down in utter dejection as they realised their fate. It was the club's first-ever relegation.

Languishing in the non-league Conference was difficult for a club that had enjoyed its 12-year stay among the country's top clubs, but with debts mounting, the club decided to sell the McCain Stadium to property developers in 2006 to stave off the debt collectors and pay for a new 4,000-seater home nearby to be ready well before the start of the 2007–08 season. This was despite the fact that Scarborough had just been relegated again to the Conference North.

Unfortunately, a feature of a bygone era prevented this – the covenant in place from the ground's creation that prevented anything other than sport on the site. Ironically for the club, this effectively ended its existence.

The club failed to convince the council that its proposals would raise enough money to both pay off the debts and build a new ground, but were given an eight-day 'stay of execution' following a change of heart. But on 20 June 2007 they were wound up in the High Court with debts of £2.5 million, ending its 128-year run as a club.

However, the winding-up of Scarborough paved the way for the supporters' trust to form a new club as Scarborough Athletic FC and secure a place in the Northern Counties East League Division One with effect from 2007–08.

The stadium remained empty and derelict, and was subject to on-going vandalism. It was further damaged by a fire on 17 October 2008 that started in the changing rooms.

In December 2008 the council finally purchased the ground from the liquidators, and Scarborough Athletic, who were forced to play away from the town, ground-sharing with Bridlington, expressed an interest in moving back to the stadium. A year later, the council announced that it had decided to invest money in a new facility rather than regenerate the stadium, and a year after that, voted to demolish the ground.

It was also revealed that Featherstone Rovers RLFC had agreed to purchase the East and West stands and undertake the demolition works that the council required for nil cost. In September 2011 the bulldozers finally moved in, completing in late November 2011. Four years later, the council granted planning permission for a supermarket to be built on the now flattened site.

Work has now commenced on the construction of multi-sport facility, Scarborough Leisure Village, at Weaponness, which will provide a new 2,000-capacity ground for Scarborough Athletic Football Club, allowing the club to 'return from exile'. It is anticipated that the construction will be completed during the

summer of 2017. The gates at the entrance to the McCain ground are to be preserved and incorporated into a new sports village complex to serve as a lasting reminder of the former Athletic Ground.

Scarborough Athletic currently compete in the eighth-tier Northern Premier League Division One North reaching the play-offs in 2016–17.

Above: The Shed Side, 1999.

Below: The old Main Stand.

Opposite: The Athletic Ground, 1960s.

Scunthorpe United   Old Show Ground

Address: Doncaster Road, Scunthorpe, North Lincolnshire DN15 7DE

Highest attendance: 23,935 v Portsmouth (FA Cup), 30 January 1954

First league match: Scunthorpe United 0-0 v Shrewsbury Town, 19 August 1950

Final league match: Scunthorpe United 1-1 v Torquay United, 18 May 1988

Ground layout: East Stand, West Stand/Main Stand, Fox Street End, Doncaster Road End

Status: Demolished

Current stadium: Glanford Park

Right: The East Stand in the 1960s.

Opposite top: The Main/West Stand.

Opposite bottom: The Doncaster Road End.

Scunthorpe United could be known as leading innovators of the British football stadium scene. During their time at the Old Show Ground they were the first team to implement the use of a cantilevered roof, producing an unobstructed view under cover for the spectators. On leaving for Glanford Park in 1988, they became the first team to relocate to a new purpose-built home since Southend United moved to Roots Hall over 30 years earlier. A significant number of teams would follow their lead.

The club had played there from their formation in 1899 and later merged with North Lindsey United, dropping Lindsey from their title in 1958. The club turned professional in 1912 and joined the Football League in 1950. They achieved promotion to the Second Division in 1958, where they stayed until 1964, but they have spent most of their time as a Football League club in the basement tier.

The Main Stand (West) that survived until the ground's demolition was constructed in 1925, after its previous incarnation was gutted by fire. The

additional roof covering the front area was added at a much later date. The original covered a very small stand that accommodated 650. The stand straddled the halfway line and there was a section of covered terrace to one side with a much lower roof, giving an overall clumsy appearance.

The Fox Street Terrace was first covered in 1938, the roof being replaced in 1959 following promotion, and its opposite number, the Doncaster Road End terrace, was covered in 1954. Both stands were of a box-like appearance with supporting pillars.

When the wooden roof of the East Stand also succumbed to fire in 1957, it was replaced by Britain's first cantilevered roof, appropriately built by the Irons' local United Steel Structural Company. This was four years before Sheffield Wednesday built a similar one at Hillsborough. The stand sat alongside the middle of the pitch with terracing either side, like the Main Stand opposite. Scunthorpe's prominent floodlights were installed in 1957 and used for the first time in a match against Rochdale in October of that year.

After the disaster at Bradford, and with new safety regulations to meet, United made the decision to sell the Old Show Ground to a supermarket chain and move to a new purpose-built but significantly smaller out-of-town stadium. Scunthorpe said goodbye to the ground by crashing out of the play-offs to Torquay United, but recent success on the pitch has brought the crowds flocking to the £2.5 million Glanford Park venue to watch Championship football.

The Old Show Ground they left behind is now a retail park. The site of the centre-spot was highlighted by a plaque in front of a supermarket delicatessen counter; however this was later removed and all that remains of the site's former use is a plaque by the entrance to the store.

The club's almost two-decade stay at Glanford Park has been eventful and has seen them play in three different divisions. They currently ply their trade in League One, reaching the play-offs in 2016–17.

Shrewsbury Town

Address: Abbey Foregate, Shrewsbury, Shropshire SY2 6AB

Highest attendance: 18,917 v Walsall, 26 April 1961

First league match: Shrewsbury Town 2-1 v Wrexham, 21 August 1950

Final league match: Shrewsbury Town 0-0 v MK Dons, 14 May 2007

International matches: England amateur (1948)

Ground layout: Main Stand, Riverside Terrace, Railway End, Wakeman End

Status: Demolished

Current stadium: The New Meadow (Greenhous Meadow)

Right: The Wakeman End.

Below: The Riverside Terrace, 1970.

Gay Meadow, its very name indicative of a golden age, was every bit as picturesque as the name suggests. Gay Meadow was known locally for the fairs, carnivals and circuses which took place there. The origin of the name is not entirely clear, although it is widely believed to be related to its use for entertainment purposes. Shrewsbury Town moved to the field by the local church on the banks of the River Severn in 1910, after being evicted from their old Copthorne Barracks home.

On arrival, a small wooden stand was constructed with basic wooden huts as dressing rooms. A revamped Main Stand was built on this side of the ground in 1922 and was extended towards the north side in 1938, where a year previously work had just been completed on what was known as the Station End, due to its close proximity to the Great Western Railway station; this was a covered stand, built over a five-year period. The initial covered centre part of the stand on the Riverside terrace was also constructed. With their prominence increasing, the club also concreted the terraces. All these developments were paid for by the supporters' club. The open opposite terrace behind the south goal was known as the Wakeman End, after the school whose windows overlooked the pitch was built behind it. Despite all these improvements Town's initial bid to join the league in 1935 was unsuccessful.

Shrewsbury's Birmingham League days had been mostly mid-table, with a few seasons challenging near

the top, the club being league champions in 1922–23. A move to the Midland Champions League in 1937–38 saw the club enjoy one of its most successful seasons, winning a league and cup treble. After a run of good seasons in post-war years, Shrewsbury were admitted to the Third Division North of the Football League in 1950, after being Midland League champions in 1949–50.

The ground did not see major improvements until the mid-1950s, when trees which lined the road to Gay Meadow (The Narrows) were felled to improve access. At around this time, the club's supporters launched a floodlight committee in order to raise £12,000 for the installation of floodlights. On the 19 November 1960 over 10,000 witnessed the turning on of the lights during the game against Queens Park Rangers. Also, dams were constructed to alleviate the problem of the bursting banks of the River Severn which, up to then, had frequently swamped Gay Meadow.

The Main Stand was covered in its entirety in 1966 when work was completed towards the Wakeman End of the ground, giving it a capacity of 18,000.

This period also saw new offices built at the club on the back of a good FA Cup run, with the Riverside terrace being renovated in the early 1970s. Named naturally because of its position close to the bank of the River Severn, the Riverside Stand was a partially covered terrace running the length of the pitch, with a refreshments bar situated halfway along the terrace and roof-mounted gantry.

In the early 1980s the club's promotion to the old Second Division required further Main Stand improvements. The old 600-seater Station End part was demolished and a new 4,500 capacity centre stand part built.

Minor changes in the 1990s included a new executive suite, the controversial demolition of the ground's wooden half-time scoreboard, and, following the Taylor Report, the removal of perimeter fencing with the exception of the Station End.

The Main Stand, 1993.

In its final years, the covered, all-seater Main Stand was split into four discrete reduced capacity enclosures: the Wakeman Stand for 1,000 home supporters, the Centre Stand for 1,000 home supporters, the Family Enclosure, a designated area for families consisting of 700 seats, and the Station Stand, a 250-capacity section for away fans.

With its postcard location, plans were made to redevelop Gay Meadow; however, with its poor access, capacity would be limited to 10,000. Added to this, the risk of potential flooding and with no room for expansion, being sandwiched between the river and a major railway junction, meant that Town, with a reduced capacity after the Taylor Report, had no choice but to move on.

In 1999 recently elected chairman Roland Wycherley released plans for a new stadium, provisionally titled the New Meadow, a 10,000 all-seater stadium on the southern outskirts of the town between the Meole Brace and Sutton Farm districts.

Amongst other factors, opposition from residents delayed the planning and building process until 2006, with the ground not being completed until July 2007. Shrewsbury played their last game at Gay Meadow, a play-off match against MK Dons, in May 2007.

Demolition of the old stadium began in September 2007, and by October the ground was reduced to rubble. Five hundred unsold seats were purchased by League of Wales side Caernarvon Town, to be used in the construction of a new stand at their ground, the Oval.

The site was sold for housing, but lay dormant due to the depressed economic climate. Finally in 2012, five years after the final game, the 179-home Riverside Meadow development, a mixture of houses and flats, began and was completed in 2016.

Shrewsbury continue to play at the New Meadow, currently named the Greenhous Meadow due to sponsorship. The Shrews currently hold a League One spot.

Southampton

Address: Milton Road, Southampton, Hampshire SO15 2XH

Highest attendance: 31,044 v Manchester United, 8 October 1969

First league match: Southampton 4–0 v Swindon Town, 30 August 1920

Final league match: Southampton 3–2 v Arsenal, 19 May 2001

Ground layout: East Stand, West Stand, Milton Road End, Archers Road End

Status: Demolished

Current stadium: St Mary's Stadium

Right: Archers Road End, 1967.

Below: West Stand, 1988.

Battling through several wartime attacks and surviving to stage Southampton's greatest games, the Dell, built in a deep hollow surrounded by trees giving the ground its name, finally succumbed to the desire for a newer stadium after 103 years, and the houses in its place now honour the club's own heroic veterans.

The Saints moved from the County Cricket Ground in 1898, as following their rapid success, and with swelling crowds, they needed a new home. The Dell was built on the site of a pond, which had to be converted into several streams that were forced underground for the stadium to be built on top. The land had been purchased from the railway, which had already cleared the area for a rail construction project that had been abandoned.

The ground initially had stands on the east and west sides flanking the pitch, with a capacity of 24,500. The other areas were natural planked banking. The terracing was surrounded by impressive solid iron railings. Finances were provided by loans and funds from the supporters' club. The Saints then joined the Football League in 1920 and a year later joined the newly-formed Football League Third Division which split into North and South sections. The 1921–22 season ended in triumph with promotion and marked the beginning of a 31-year stay in the Second Division.

Both stands would not last long, however, as the west was replaced in 1925 with a double-decker structure designed by Archibald Leitch that largely survived until the Dell's final day, while the east was ravaged by fire four years later, a slightly smaller mirror image double-decker facility rapidly emerging in its place.

The Dell's proximity to Southampton docks meant the stadium was always at risk of attack during the Second World War, and on 30 November 1940 a bomb struck the ground towards the Milton Road End,

causing a giant 18ft crater in the penalty area that exposed one of the underground streams, resulting in major flooding.

An armaments explosion in the West Stand in March 1941 also caused significant damage, though the resulting fire was rapidly doused. The damage was repaired quite quickly, but Southampton played the majority of their wartime games away from home.

To accommodate a post-war boom in attendances, the club created a two-tiered uncovered terrace on the Milton Road End by building platforms on top of the existing banking. These became known as the 'chocolate boxes' and lasted until the 1980s. Both end terraces at the stadium were distinctive, as public roads running behind them caused the ground to look like a parallelogram owing to their slanting nature.

In 1950 the Dell became the first ground in England to have permanent floodlighting installed. The first game played under the lights was a 60-minute friendly on 31 October against Bournemouth & Boscombe Athletic. The football establishment however was less enthusiastic. Following the first competitive football match to be played under lights, a Football Combination (reserve) fixture between Saints and Tottenham Hotspur on the evening of 1 October 1951 in front of almost 14,000, the FA and the Football League called a moratorium on their use. It was not until 1955 that they were 'legalised', but then only for re-arranged fixtures.

By 1960, when the Saints had returned to the Second Division, floodlit football was no longer a novelty. The Dell's lighting system was radically modernised by the addition of catwalks and light mountings across the stand roofs. These were upgraded again in 1966 on the club's promotion to the First Division. In the Dell's confined space, there was no room for corner pylons.

The chocolate boxes were taken down in the 1980s and replaced by a new stand used for family ticket holders. This was a two-level concrete structure, which became affectionately known as the 'The Piano Lid'.

The standing areas under the East and West stands were fitted with bench seats in the late 1970s, before the Dell became an all-seater stadium in the early 1990s in the wake of the Hillsborough disaster. New roofed stands were erected at both ends of the stadium, one replacing the Milton Road End family stand which was just a few years old and the other a rudimentary affair on the Archers Road End which came to be known affectionately as The Bikeshed. This reduced the stadium's capacity to a mere 15,000, the smallest in the top division at the time.

Even before Taylor, the cluttered city-centre site, with no room for expansion and difficult to modernise, had the club's directors desperately searching for an alternative home. With Southampton annually scraping survival in the Premier League, the decision was made in 1998 to move away in 2001 to the £32 million St Mary's Stadium on the banks of the River Itchen.

The Dell was rapidly demolished and converted into housing, with all the apartment blocks bearing the names of former club legends like Matt Le Tissier and Mick Channon, so at least some connection remains.

The time at St Mary's has been a rocky one; the club lost its Premier League status in 2005 and subsequent events saw the club enter into administration in 2009 and drop into League One. However, the club has since fully regained that lost ground, and the 2016–17 season has seen both Premier League and Europa League football at Southampton.

Milton Road End before the covered stand.

Southport

Haig Avenue

Address: Haig Avenue, Blowick, Southport, Lancashire PR8 6LD

Highest attendance: 20,111 v Newcastle United, (FA Cup), 26 January 1932

First league match: Southport 1-1 v Durham City, 27 August 1921

Final league match: Southport 1-1 v Huddersfield Town, 22 April 1978

International matches: England Youth

Other usages: Liverpool Reserves, Everton Reserves

Ground layout: Main Stand, Popular Side, The Scarisbrick New Road End/The Jack Carr Stand, The Blowick Road End

Status: Extant

Current stadium: Haig Avenue (Merseyrail Community Stadium)

Right: Main Stand, September 1969.

Opposite above: The Popular Side, 1997.

Opposite below: The old Scarisbrick New Road End, September 1969.

Alongside Anfield, Goodison Park and Prenton Park, Southport FC's Haig Avenue stadium comprised a quartet of Football League grounds in Merseyside for a large part of the 20th century before they lost their league status in 1978. Opened in 1905, the ground and the road it was on were originally christened Ash Lane before being renamed in honour of Earl Haig, coinciding with Southport's election to the Football League in 1921 as founder members of the Football League Third Division North.

A wooden grandstand, purchased from the Southport Flower Show, pre-dated Southport's election to the league, having been relocated from their former home on Scarisbrick New Road, but the new era was celebrated by a covered terrace erected opposite on the Popular Side, running the full length of the pitch. In 1932 it was extended around the east side of the ground to the Scarisbrick New Road End.

In this era came the club's FA Cup run of 1930–31, where Haig Avenue witnessed a fifth-round victory over Bradford Park

Avenue that set up a Merseyside derby quarter-final against Everton.

The original floodlights were built in 1961 along the sides of the pitch and were first used in an FA Cup match with Shrewsbury Town on 9 January 1962, Southport being one of the last league clubs to install lights. Their design was overhauled just a few years later during Billy Bingham's successful spell as manager of the club. Two more bulbs were added to each pylon to increase the brightness for any possible television coverage.

Amongst Bingham's other ideas to increase awareness was the erection of a set of flagpoles behind the Blowick terrace, similar to those in place at Fulham's Craven Cottage at the time.

An all-too-common culprit, a carelessly discarded cigarette butt, was suspected to have caused Haig Avenue's original wooden grandstand to perish in flames on Boxing Day 1966. Most of the club's possessions, including kits, went up in flames and only the club safe (holding the previous day's takings) survived. A Fire Disaster Appeal Fund was set up in the weeks following the blaze with an initial target of £70,000 set to raise money for a replacement. However, it was wound up after a year having raised only £10,000.

A temporary main stand was put up instead during the season Billy Bingham's side won promotion to the Third Division in 1967. Replaced two years later the Grandstand, as it's called, still survives today. This covered all-seated stand houses around 1,800 supporters. The stand doesn't run the full length of the pitch and straddles the halfway line, with the spaces on either side unused by spectators.

In the late 1970s the state of the terracing, much like the fortunes of the club, had already gone into decline and part of the Popular Side terrace had already been fenced off on safety grounds, and 1978 saw Southport drop out of the Football League, narrowly losing a re-election vote to Wigan Athletic. They were the last club to leave the Football League through the re-election process. The club declined to enter the forerunner to the Conference, electing instead to join the lower Northern Premier League.

In the wake of the Bradford fire, the covered terracing running along the Popular Side, as well as that at the Scarisbrick Road End, was demolished in 1986, leaving the ground a sorry sight. This action was forced upon the club following legal action by Sefton Council under the Safety of Sports Grounds legislation.

Many supporters today still feel aggrieved that instead of assisting the club to build new covered terracing, their council took such harsh action against Southport when it was already going through a difficult period. Following the demolition, grass banks and a few steps of terracing were all that remained on two sides of the stadium. On the other, three giant pillars

remained behind the Scarisbrick New Road End goal, as a lasting memory of the old stand. These were eventually removed during the rebuilding exercise in the early 1990s.

The 1992–93 season saw Southport pushing for promotion to the Conference and due to the stricter ground grading criteria at the higher level, the club built new uncovered terracing around the Popular Side and Blowick Road End, along with a new covered terrace at the Scarisbrick New Road End of the stadium. This stand was renamed the Jack Carr Stand, in honour and memory of the former club director and president.

In the late 1990s further terracing was added to the Blowick and Popular sides of the stadium, and the white perimeter wall, built by Billy Bingham's squad as part of pre-season training in the 1960s, was replaced by a metal fence following the introduction of new ruling governing the height of pitch-side fences. A small section of the white wall has been kept as a reminder of the hard work of Bingham's men.

Southport's main non-league achievement followed in 1998 with the FA Trophy final, with a decent local following travelling to Wembley to witness a brave but single-goal defeat at the hands of Cheltenham Town.

The ground now appears as follows. The Popular Side still remains uncovered and is unusual in the respect that this stand is comprised of four separate blocks. The covered Jack Carr Stand is where the majority of the home fans congregate. This terrace can house just over 900 fans. The roof has no supporting pillars to hinder the view, but only runs for around half the width of the playing area. The roof only partially covers the stand. The Blowick Road End for away supporters is a small open terrace; this runs the width of the pitch and is divided into three sub-terraces, with two small terraced areas either side of the larger terraced area.

On 10 September 2012 it was announced that Merseyrail had agreed a sponsorship deal that would see Haig Avenue renamed the Merseyrail Community

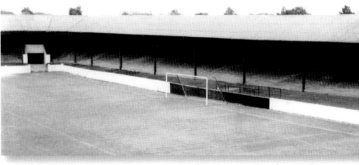

Stadium. In the summer of 2014 and into 2015, with the financial assistance of 'Trust in Yellow' (the Supporters' Trust), County Insurance and a grant from the football authorities, the club erected new corner floodlights to replace those put up along the sides of the pitch over 40 years previously.

While never quite reaching the heights of their Merseyside neighbours, Southport enjoyed an eventful league existence, fluctuating between the Third and Fourth Divisions. They have slowly forced their way back up the leagues and were one promotion away from a return to the Football League in 2015–16. Sadly, this momentum was halted in 2016–17, with the club relegated from the National League.

Stockport County

Address: Hardcastle Road, Edgeley, Stockport, Cheshire SK3 9DD

Highest attendance: 27,833 v Liverpool (FA Cup), 11 February 1950

First league match: Stockport County 1-1 v Gainsborough Trinity, 13 September 1902

Final league match: Stockport County 1-1 v Cheltenham Town, 7 May 2011

Ground-sharing: Sale Sharks

Other usages: Lacrosse

Ground layout: Main Stand/Danny Bergara Stand, Popular Side/Vernon Stand, Railway End, Cheadle End

Status: Extant

Current stadium: Edgeley Park

Right: Cheadle End, August 1969.

Opposite top: The Popular Side, 1988, after conversion to seats.

Opposite bottom: The Main Stand, 1988.

The club's nomadic existence was brought to an end in 1902 when Stockport County moved to Edgeley Park from Green Lane, needing to find a bigger stadium to play in following their entrance into the Second Division of the Football League two years earlier. County moved in with the local rugby league club and have stayed ever since. The rugby club ceased to exist after 1902.

A year after moving in, a new covered stand was constructed on the Popular Side of the ground, housing 1,400 supporters. A decade later came the first major development: the Main Stand was built, a 500-seater low timber enclosure which incorporated new changing rooms and office accommodation.

A further decade on, a largely wooden terrace was built at the Cheadle End with room for around 3,000.

During 1927 the Popular Side was reconstructed, and in 1934 it was extended further back to hold 16,000. The stand now ran the whole length of the terracing.

In the summer of 1935 the Main Stand burned down. It was rebuilt just a year later. Constructed of brick and steel, it was a building seen by many as a traditional, old-fashioned stand, typical of stadia in Northern England. This roof was supported towards the front by three steel columns. Unusually, rather than running the length of the pitch, the Main Stand was only about 75 yards long, straddling the halfway line, with the gaps at each end containing other club-related buildings. It survives in pretty much the same form today.

Just after the war, the ground saw the longest-ever football match ever played. Stockport County played against Doncaster Rovers on 30 March 1946 in a Third Division North cup tie. The match was deadlocked at 2–2 at 90 minutes, and after two 10-minute periods of extra time there was no further score. The rule at that time was that the game would carry on until one team scored. However, after 203 minutes and with darkness closing in, the game was finally stopped.

In 1950 a record crowd of 27,833 crammed into Edgeley Park to watch a fifth-round FA Cup game against Liverpool who edged the tie 2–1.

In 1954 the roof on the Popular Side was extended forward to cover the whole terrace. On completion, the stand was renamed the Barlow Stand to commemorate the sterling work undertaken by Ernest Barlow, the club chairman from 1923 until his death 31 years later. As with the Main Stand opposite, the roof was supported towards the front by several steel columns.

The floodlighting system cost £17,000 and the funds were raised by the supporters and were first used in a friendly match against Fortuna '54 Geleen of Holland on 16 October 1956. The visitors included four members of the Dutch national team that had defeated Belgium the previous week. Stockport won 3–0 in front of a crowd of 14,511.

The ground once held two matches on the same day by the England international football team. On 14 January 1958 the England squad were due to play training matches at nearby Maine Road, but their pitch was frozen. Edgeley Park's pitch was deemed playable and so it was decided to hold the matches in Stockport instead. The first game saw England draw 2–2 with a Manchester City XI, and the second saw the England senior side defeat the England U-23 side 1–0.

In 1967 basic bench seating was installed in the Cheadle End, reducing the capacity to 1,100.

In 1978 Edgeley Park was the venue for the championship and final of the World Lacrosse tournament, contested by England, Canada, the USA and Australia. That same year, the Barlow Stand terracing at the rear of the stand was dismantled and levelled and the capacity was halved as it was replaced by an all-weather five-a-side pitch.

By the mid-1980s, three changes occurred. Firstly, the old wooden sleepers at the open Railway End were replaced with concrete terracing. Secondly, changes were made to the Main Stand that saw the

paddock, a terrace well below pitch level in front of the seated area, filled with concrete and fitted with blue plastic seats. Similar seats replaced the old, uncomfortable wooden seats in the stand soon after. This modernisation, unfortunately, necessitated the removal of the unique Edgeley Park drawbridge. This timber structure was lowered to provide access for the players from the tunnel, over the paddock, and onto the pitch. Thirdly, the wooden Cheadle End was demolished following the Bradford disaster and replaced by just seven shallow steps of concrete terracing.

A decade later in 1994 the Popular Side was made all-seater, its capacity thereby being reduced to 2,411. A year later came the largest development with a new 5,000-seat-capacity Cheadle End stand. The two-tiered large structure had room for conference and banqueting suites as well as shop facilities. The stand was by far the largest and most modern in the stadium. It was one of the largest Kop stands outside the Premier League.

In 2001, 1,300 seats were bolted on to the Railway End terrace as Football League rules required stadia to be all-seated in the top two divisions of English football. This was the last part of Edgeley Park to be converted to seating, thus making the ground compliant. The terrace was still open to the elements.

Around the turn of the century, the County chairman announced plans to rebuild the Railway End. The plan would have involved purchasing The Bungalow behind it, on which a hotel would have been built, which would have overlooked the ground. However, like other Millennium-related projects, these plans never came to fruition.

In 2003 the ground was shared with Sale Sharks rugby union club, a relationship that was to last until 2012.

That same year, the Main Stand was renamed the Danny Bergara Stand, in honour of the club's former and late manager who led County to remarkable success in the early 1990s, including four visits to

Wembley. In July 2015 Stockport Council purchased the stadium for around £2 million, leasing it back to the football club on a commercial basis, in order to prevent it from being demolished and redeveloped.

Sadly, the last 15 years have proved disastrous for the team. The historic side were playing second-tier football as late as 2002, but have since suffered four relegations which now see them as a semi-professional club competing in the sixth-tier National League North.

Stoke City

Victoria Ground

Stoke City stayed at their Victoria Ground stadium for 119 years – an English record only surpassed by Wolverhampton Wanderers' stay at Molineux. City themselves are also considered the country's second oldest league football team after Notts County – both the club and its home are integral parts of the British game. The ground took its name from the nearby Victoria Hotel.

The club switched to the site from the adjacent Sweeting's Fields in 1878 as Stoke FC, having changed their name from Stoke Ramblers. The site was originally a large oval expanse of banking, built to accommodate a running track used by the local athletics club, with just one small, compact wooden stand on the east side (Boothen Road), capable of housing 1,000 people.

Stoke's early years saw them drop in and out of league competition, with their home ground declared as one of the poorest in the Football League. But when they returned for the second time in 1919, the club, who by now owned the ground, had been forced into action and they now possessed another small wooden stand, this time on the Butler Street side.

During the early 1920s a rebuilt mainly wooden Main Stand was erected and this could hold 2,000 fans. By 1930 Stoke had added City to their name and the Boothen End was terraced and later covered with a roof with a number of supporting pillars running across the stand's middle. As a consequence, the ground lost its oval shape.

In 1935, with the likes of a young Stanley Matthews beginning to draw in the crowds, the Butler Street Stand was rebuilt with an impressive barrel roof, giving seating to 5,000 people. In front of the seats was a small paddock, with room for another 2,000, and it took the ground capacity to around the 45,000 mark. The stand would ultimately have a row of executive boxes constructed across the back. On 29 March 1937 a record crowd of 51,380 packed into the Victoria Ground to watch a First Division match against Arsenal.

1956 saw the installation of floodlights, with fierce local rivals Port Vale being the visitors in a Second

Open Stoke End and Butler Street Stand, 1966.

Division clash to declare them switched on. The Valiants were left in the shadows of their opponents though, as Stoke ran out 3–1 winners in front of a bumper crowd of almost 39,000.

Beginning in 1960 another replacement two-tiered covered Main Stand was built in three phases over three years and the dressing rooms were revamped. In the summer of 1963 concrete was laid on the paddock terracing of the stand and it was the Stoke players who helped lay it as part of a team bonding scheme.

Over a weekend in January 1976, with Stoke playing Tottenham Hotspur away in the FA Cup, winds of almost hurricane intensity battered Stoke-on-Trent. The strong winds blew a section of the roof from the Butler Street Stand leaving only the west corner intact. The top priority was to put the roof back in order, so that the replay against Tottenham could take place on 7 January.

However, on the day of the match, as workmen were replacing timber supports and erecting scaffolding, some of the supports collapsed and a number of workers were injured. The match itself was cancelled on safety grounds. Stoke had to play

one home league match, against Middlesbrough, at Vale Park on 17 January and the Victoria Ground was reopened by 24 January in time for Stoke to play Tottenham. The repair proved to be very costly for Stoke as prized playing assets had to be sold on to balance the books.

As the 1980s approached, work was completed on a two-tiered Stoke End behind the goal, seating 4,000 spectators. This replaced the former huge open terrace. This stand also had seating to the rear and terracing to the front.

The final improvements to the ground were made during the 1980s with the Stanley Matthews Suite being opened as well as a new club shop and offices. The suite was located on the corner of the Boothen End and the Boothen Stand.

Twice in the 1980s the club were unsuccessful in obtaining planning permission for a supermarket on the site, which would have led to a ground-share with Port Vale. Despite the recommendations of the Taylor Report in the 1990s, the Victoria Ground looked well-equipped to adapt, and plans for a £5 million ground redevelopment were drawn up. It appeared as if Stoke City would stay for many more years to come,

but in 1996 the decision was made by chief executive Jez Moxey to move to a state-of-the-art 28,000-seater ground, the Britannia Stadium, at nearby Trentham Lakes costing £14.7 million.

The ground was completely demolished soon after the final game and at the time of its demolition it was the oldest ground in the Football League. Almost two decades on, the land on which the ground stood still lies derelict, which is allegedly due to the recession and 'numerous other factors'. The council rejected plans for office development, but the property company who purchased it still hopes to put housing on the site in the near future.

The first season at the Britannia saw Stoke City sink into the third tier of English football, but they gradually recovered and returned to the Premier League stage in 2008 where they have consolidated, and the new ground has also hosted European football.

Above left: Main Stand, 1988.

Above: The Stoke End.

Sunderland

Address: Grantham Road, Roker, Sunderland SR6 9SW

Highest attendance: 75,118 v Derby County (FA Cup), 8 March 1933

First league match: Sunderland 1-0 v Liverpool, 10 September 1898

Final league match: Sunderland 3-0 v Everton, 3 May 1997

International matches: The World Cup (1966)

Ground layout: Main Stand, Clock Stand, Fulwell End, Roker End

Status: Demolished

Current stadium: Stadium of Light

Right: The Main Stand, 1974.

Opposite: Fulwell End, 1988.

Sunderland's stay at Roker Park ended in 1997, just one year shy of a century. Yet its trophy cabinet was always well stocked, Sunderland obtaining no less than 10 pieces of silverware while at their home. The Wearsiders were elected to the First Division in 1890–91, replacing founder members Stoke. They won the league title the following year and repeated the feat the following season. From 1886 until 1898, Sunderland's home ground was in Newcastle Road.

Within a year of the farmland being leased in 1898, Roker Park had been built, with the initial wooden stands taking only three months to construct. The stadium had two basic stands when Sunderland moved in: a single-tier grandstand with a paddock at the front with a 3,000 capacity and the original standing-only Clock Stand having 32 steep steps and housing an impressive 15,500. In 1908 Sunderland purchased the land.

In 1912 the open Roker End, previously a wooden terrace, was enlarged using an intricate arrangement of concrete beams to support it, a unique feature that would last for 70 years. The original turf was brought from Ireland, and lasted for 38 years. The pitch was designed to have a slight drop of about one foot from the centre of the pitch to each corner to help with drainage.

The Fulwell End was expanded in 1925 on a plain earth bank, and in 1929 the old wooden grandstand (President Stand) was demolished and Archibald Leitch was brought in to design Roker Park's new grandstand, giving the stadium a capacity of 60,000. The typical steel criss-cross lattice work used on the balcony can still be seen today at Ibrox (Glasgow Rangers), and Goodison Park (Everton). The financial undertaking on the new Main Stand, costing almost £25,000, nearly bankrupted the club. Seven years later, the Leitch-designed Clock Stand was constructed, being 375ft long in two sections.

During the Second World War, a bomb landed on the middle of the pitch, and a similar device fell in the car park, damaging the old clubhouse on the corner of Roker Baths Road. However, this did little to halt the continuing work at Roker Park. In 1950, the shelf

was added to the Main Stand between the top seats and the paddock standing area, giving it a three-tier look.

In 1952 Roker Park was fitted with floodlights, being only the second ground in the country to do so after Arsenal's Highbury Stadium. They were first used in a friendly against Dundee. The lights were only a temporary addition, and were replaced by permanent structures at the end of the season after proving to be a success.

In 1966 Roker Park was selected as a World Cup venue ahead of St James' Park. Sunderland received substantial grants and loans from the Football Association as a result. The pitch had to be extended by three yards and extra temporary seating was installed in the Clock Stand; the Fulwell End was also covered in anticipation. The ground in general was given a facelift and a necessary television gantry was installed. During the World Cup, three group matches and the quarter-final between the Soviet Union and Hungary (2–1) were played at the ground.

During the 1970s there were even more improvements to Roker Park, some of these being financed by their popular 1973 FA Cup final victory. These improvements included the installation of underground sprinklers, the upgrading of the floodlights to European Standards and the re-sheeting of the roofs. Also a row of 14 executive boxes was added on the middle tier of the Main Stand.

The 1980s saw a downturn in the club's fortunes, and the stadium began to decay. The part-demolition of the still uncovered Roker End in 1982 as the concrete began to crumble was the beginning of the end for the stadium. The Taylor Report in 1989 dictated that it needed to become all-seater, but meeting this requirement would have decreased its capacity severely, a constraint unacceptable for a club competing in the top division.

The ground was too expensive to repair and too confined for expansion, being hemmed in by housing, and so the chairman decided to take advantage of

an EEC grant and look for a site for a new stadium. In 1992 plans were unveiled to build a 48,000-seat stadium close to the Nissan car factory, which would be part of a mega leisure complex, but Nissan objected to such a site being developed near to their headquarters.

Instead, five years later in 1997, Sunderland moved to the 42,000-capacity Stadium of Light, in nearby Monkwearmouth, on the site of the closed Monkwearmouth Colliery. A section of the old Leitch lattice work can still be seen in the main car park of the Stadium of Light.

Roker Park was demolished and in its place was built a housing estate. At the time of demolition, apart

from the Roker End, the stands and ends remained largely intact from the time of Archibald Leitch's construction of them, a tribute to his design skills. Thankfully, to commemorate Roker Park, the new streets were named Promotion Close, Clockstand Close, Goalmouth Close, Midfield Drive, Turnstile Mews and Roker Park Close.

In the two decades since leaving Roker, the Black Cats have spent the majority of the time gracing the Premier League. Following a disappointing campaign in 2016–17, Sunderland were relegated back to the Championship.

Swansea City

Vetch Field

Address: Glamorgan Street, Swansea, West Glamorgan SA1 3SU

Highest attendance: 32,796 v Arsenal (FA Cup), 17 February 1968

First league match: Swansea City 2-1 v Watford, 2 September 1920

Final league match: Swansea City 1-0 v Shrewsbury, 30 April 2005

International matches: Wales (Football), Wales (Rugby League)

Other usages: Rugby League, Rock Concerts

Ground layout: North Bank, South/Centre Stand, East Stand, West Stand

Status: Demolished

Current stadium: Liberty Stadium

Right: West Stand, 1979.

Opposite top: South/Centre Stand, 1992.

Opposite below: North Bank, 1992.

Named after the cabbage-like legume that grew on the site, Vetch Field became the home of Swansea Town from their formation in 1912, having previously played host to amateur outfit Swansea Villa. The site, also known as The Old Town Ditch Field, was in essence a piece of waste ground owned by Swansea Gaslight Company. The site was in a good location and deemed surplus to requirements by the company, so the club moved in, purchasing the ground.

The first 1,500-capacity Main Stand with a gable and clock was erected in the south at the beginning of the club's tenancy before the stadium even had turf; it was originally a grassless compacted coal cinder surface.

The club spent a few seasons in the Southern League, before becoming founder members of the Third Division in 1920.

After the club had established the pitch, in 1925 the North Bank was terraced. Two years later, the first incarnation of the two-tier West Stand behind the goal was built with a capacity for 2,000 people, with bench seating above the terracing. The remaining side had just a mound where more people could attend games.

It would be another three decades before more stands would join it, the supporters paying £16,000 for the North Bank terracing to be covered with a low roof supported by several pillars before floodlights were installed a year later in 1960, with Hibernian the visitors for a friendly.

This preceded Swansea, renamed City in 1970, plummeting from the old Second Division towards the Football League trapdoor, finishing bottom of all 92 clubs in 1975 but gaining a reprieve through

re-election. During this time, they sold the ground to the council. Happier times at the Vetch Field followed, as they rocketed from the basement tier to the top of the entire Football League in just over three years under former Welsh international John Toshack.

In the late 1970s Swansea started a redevelopment programme which resulted in the construction of a double-decker seated stand in place of the concrete and wooden sleeper East terraces, costing £800,000. A small layer of steep terracing lay beneath the stand with a capacity of around 2,500. Due to objections raised by the residents living in William Street behind the stand, it could only be constructed over two-thirds of the pitch width; it opened in early 1981.

The East Stand was also home to one of the strangest floodlights in the league, jutting out over the stand, seemingly completely out of character with the rest of the ground. There were further plans for this stand to wrap around and replace the dilapidated Main Stand (now Centre Stand), largely unaltered since its construction in 1912, but the money never materialised to complete this task or, ultimately, any further major ground development. However, another £700,000 was needed just for basic ground maintenance and safety.

The late 1980s and early 1990s saw the second tier of the West Stand closed and then built over amid safety concerns in the wake of the Hillsborough and Bradford disasters. Further safety concerns reduced the North Bank capacity with a large section at the rear being blocked off, and following Hillsborough its safety certificate was again cut, and by the early 21st century the stand held around just 3,500.

These were early indicators that the Vetch Field may have no longer been suited to Swansea City, and even though the club resided in England's lower leagues at that time, plans were made for the construction of a new stadium.

The 1990s saw the Vetch Field also used for rugby league with several Wales international matches being played there and also the occasional club rugby match.

Expansion of the Vetch was never a realistic option due to the proximity of housing and the sea. In 2005 the club left their home to take up residence in a new purpose-built arena, The Liberty Stadium, shared with the Ospreys Rugby Union Club. The new home replaced an old athletics stadium on the same site.

The Vetch Field infrastructure remained untouched for six years after the club's departure. The site had initially been destined to be turned into a community centre and housing estate, but these plans never materialised. The ground lay derelict until early 2011 when it was finally demolished over a six-month period. During this hiatus, the pitch had been used as community allotments and there remained a strong local feeling that the ground and surrounds should be kept as an 'urban utopia'. After another five-year delay, an agreed way forward has been thrashed out.

Ultimately the 'Sandfields' site will allow open spaces for children, and 40 new houses arranged in short terraces alongside sheltered housing for the elderly. There will be a community orchard where

apple and other fruit trees will be grown. The old centre circle of The Vetch will be retained, as this is where people's ashes have been spread. This will become a wild flower meadow.

Since moving, the club have fought themselves up from League One to become in 2012 the first Welsh club to compete in the Premier League, a place they continue to hold.

Torquay United

Address: Plainmoor, Torquay, Devon TQ1 3PS

Highest attendance: 21,908 v Huddersfield Town (FA Cup), 29 January 1955

First league match: Torquay United 1-1 v Exeter City, 27 August 1927

Final league match: Torquay United 0-3 v Wycombe Wanderers, 3 May 2014

Ground layout: The Grandstand/Paul Bristow Stand, The Popular Side, Ellacombe End/Cowshed, Babbacombe End

Status: Extant

Current stadium: Plainmoor (The Launa Windows Stadium)

Below: Babbacombe End, 1996.

Opposite above: The old Popular side, 1987.

Opposite below: Ellacombe End/Family Stand newly built, 1993.

After a nomadic start that had seen Torquay play at the Torquay Cricket Ground, the club moved to Plainmoor in 1910 which had been first used for athletics and rugby as early as 1881. Torquay merged with rivals Ellacombe FC to become Torquay Town. Initially Plainmoor was shared with another rival, Babbacombe, and pressure began to mount in favour of Torquay Town and Babbacombe coming together. This was because at the end of the First World War, the first teams of Exeter City and Plymouth Argyle were promoted from the Southern League into the newly-formed Third Division South. Torquay Town and Babbacombe finally became Torquay United in 1921.

There was a rudimentary structure in existence on Plainmoor in 1892. A second wooden grandstand was constructed alongside the original during the first season after merger. Six years later, Torquay won election to the Third Division South of the Football League and immediately purchased a stand costing £150, ready for United's inaugural season in the Football League; the stand had previously stood at Buckfastleigh Racecourse, where its derelict twin can still be seen today at the long-closed venue. The stand replaced the two previous structures. The roof of the stand was blown off during a gale three years later and the infrastructure damaged.

Other improvements followed, including banked terracing parallel to Marnham Road. This became known as the Popular Side. The following year the Cowshed was constructed behind the Ellacombe End goal.

Very little changed for the next 30 years, as the ground saw generations of supporters move through its turnstiles. In 1953 a roof was placed over a large section of the Popular Side. During the 1954–55 season almost 22,000 fans watched Torquay's 0–1 defeat at the hands of Huddersfield Town in the FA Cup. The same season also saw United become one of the first lower division clubs to introduce floodlights to their ground. These were only good enough for friendly matches and were soon replaced by Football League standard floodlighting, and these were first used in December 1960.

The following close season, the grandstand, long repaired after the serious storm damage in 1930, was extended in the direction of the Ellacombe end of the ground.

In December 1962 the middle section of the Cowshed collapsed under the weight of snow, and so four years later the Mini-Stand, comprising covered standing accommodation, was built behind that Ellacombe End goal. Finally, four years after that, the final section of the previous Cowshed was badly damaged by storms and demolished, as it

was now unsafe, and the Mini-Stand was eventually extended in its place.

1984 prompted a few cosmetic changes to the terracing, but on 16 May 1985, just six days after the Bradford stadium fire, a third of the old grandstand was destroyed during an early morning blaze. Nobody was hurt, but as a result the ground's capacity fell to below 5,000. In the few years after the fire, the ground saw little change. At one point, the manager's office and changing rooms were situated in a couple of portable cabins behind the old Mini-Stand. This part of the stand was re-roofed and repaired.

However, during the late 1980s and throughout the 1990s, Plainmoor finally saw some major changes. In 1992 the old Mini-Stand was demolished and made way for the all-seater Family Stand, which also housed offices, the boardroom and the club shop, as well as the pub and restaurant.

In 1994 the old railway-sleeper terracing on the Popular Side was replaced by narrower steeper terracing with a roof running the length of the side of the ground, with a bowling club and a car park built behind the terracing. Later this would include a television gantry.

The last side of the ground to be covered was the open Babbacombe End, normally the away end. This was redeveloped incorporating a roof in 2000 and initially called the Sparkworld Stand.

In 2007 Torquay United were relegated from the Football League after 80 years. However, they bounced back after only two years at Conference level. The main stand that was originally from Buckfastleigh Racecourse was demolished in the autumn of 2011 and accordingly the ground capacity was reduced. A new 1,750-seat stand filling the complete length of the pitch was erected during the season and opened in August 2012 in time for the start of the following season. It was named Bristow's Bench after the late former director Paul Bristow, who so generously supported the club after

a lottery win. Regrettably, United hit another bad patch and lost Football League status for a second time in May 2014.

On 15 September 2014 Torquay United announced a four-year deal with local company Launa Windows to rename Plainmoor The Launa Windows Stadium in an effort to increase revenue.

At the time of writing, the freehold of Plainmoor is on the table as Torquay United move into the final stages of a long-awaited takeover. On the pitch events have not significantly improved, with Torquay in mid-table of the National League, which is a shame as this pretty soccer outpost is a popular visit for any away fan.

Tranmere Rovers

Prenton Park

Address: Prenton Road West, Prenton, Wirral CH42 9PY

Highest attendance: 24,424 v Stoke City (FA Cup), 5 February 1972

First league match: Tranmere Rovers 4–1 v Crewe Alexandra, 27 August 1921

Final league match: Tranmere Rovers 0–1 v Bury, 2 May 2015

Other usages: Liverpool Reserves

Ground layout: The Main Stand, The Bebington Kop, Borough Road Stand/The John King Stand, The Cowshed

Status: Extant

Current stadium: Prenton Park

Formed in 1884, Tranmere played their first matches at Steele's Field in Birkenhead, but in 1887 they bought a new site from the Tranmere Rugby Club. Although that ground was not strictly in Prenton, it was given the name as it was considered more upmarket. As that land was eventually required for housing, shops and a school as Birkenhead expanded in 1912, Rovers transferred lock, stock and barrel to their third home on the corner of Prenton Road West and Borough Road, taking the ground name with it.

The present Prenton Park was opened on 9 March 1912. Following the expansion of the Football League in 1921 to the Third Division North and South, Rovers were accepted into the Third Division North and played their first fixture against Crewe Alexandra at Prenton Park on 27 August 1921, winning 4–1. Upon this elevation, an old wooden stand was transported from the nearby Oval sports ground, and a stand was also put up on the other side, though the remainder was open terraces. The Prenton Park ground failed to emerge from the Second World War unscathed due to

the bombing of Birkenhead. The cover on the Borough Road side was destroyed, but it was replaced after the war. In 1956 The Cowshed was built, with five discrete gabled sections.

Floodlights were installed at the ground in September 1958 and used in a match against Rochdale. The supporters' association raised the £15,000 cost of the new lights. When manager Dave Russell joined the club in 1961, one of his many influential changes was to take advantage of the lights, regularly playing home games on Friday nights rather than the usual Saturday afternoon. This allowed supporters to watch Tranmere on Fridays and First Division sides Everton or Liverpool on Saturdays. The idea was successful and continued until the 1990s.

By 1968 the existing old wooden Main Stand was in poor condition and in need of replacement. At a cost of £80,000 the current Main Stand was erected and opened by Minister for Sport and former referee Denis Howell. It had a capacity of 5,957 and was a two-tier stand, divided into three main sections. The lower tier

Right: Borough Road Stand, 1970.

Opposite above: The Main Stand in the 1970s, newly built.

Opposite below: Cowshed, 1967. The original structure with five gables.

consisted of the Bebington/Kop End paddock (capacity 1,150) and the Town/Cowshed End paddock (capacity 1,209), either side of the halfway line. The upper tier is simply referred to as the Main Stand (capacity 3,598).

Four years later the ground's largest-ever crowd of 24,424 packed in for a 1972 FA Cup match between Tranmere and Stoke City. In 1979 the terracing on The Cowshed and paddocks were concreted. The Cowshed roof had also been replaced during the 1970s following a gale, this time with three gabled sections. The Tranmere suite was added to the Main Stand in 1988, with further bars and executive suites added soon after. The stand is now almost 50 years old and is becoming increasingly costly and difficult to maintain.

Many improvements to the ground were driven by changes in legislation. In 1985 the Safety of Sports Grounds Act led to a reduction in capacity from 18,000 to 8,000. The Kop End was closed and the Main Stand was partially closed, reducing its capacity by 3,000, because there were insufficient access points. £50,000 was then spent on safety work, including fireproofing the Main Stand, to maintain the capacity at 8,000, but the club were unable to afford any further refurbishment. This meant the leaking Borough Road stand roof remained in poor condition.

Sections of the ground's exterior land were also sold off to private companies. On the positive side, the floodlights were replaced. In dire financial trouble in 1987, the club went into administration and Prenton Park looked destined to become yet another supermarket. Thankfully, following a takeover by Peter Johnson, a rosier picture emerged.

However, the biggest changes of all took place during 1994 and 1995. The Taylor Report required that all stadia in the top two divisions should be all seated, and the club's response was to completely redevelop three sides of the ground with entirely new all-seater stands created – the Borough Road Stand, The Cowshed and the new Kop. Capacity in the ground thus increased to the 16,600 that it is today. The Main Stand was also upgraded. On 11

March 1995 the 'new ground' was officially opened at a cost of £3.1 million.

The Bebington Kop, simply referred to as the Kop, was a large single-tier, all-seater stand with a capacity of 5,696. It replaced the earlier open terrace. The Bebington Kop was also the biggest Kop stand in non-league football, outstripping the entire capacity of a number of non-league grounds and a few league grounds too. Originally the stand housed both home and away fans, but in 2001 the Kop was given over entirely to the home fans.

The Johnny King Stand was formerly known as the Borough Road Stand, but was renamed in 2002 to recognise former Rovers manager John King. The stand ran along the Borough Road side of the pitch, and was a low-rise seated stand with a capacity of 2,414.

The Cowshed had a capacity of 2,500. It possessed a slanted seating arrangement, caused by the main road running behind it.

However, these ground enhancements were just a prelude to the most successful period in Tranmere's history; under manager John King, the team reached the play-offs for promotion to the Premier League in three successive seasons between 1993 and 1995. Under King's successor, John Aldridge, Tranmere experienced a number of cup runs, most notably reaching the 2000 Football League Cup Final. Other cup runs include reaching FA Cup quarter-finals in 2000, 2001 and 2004. Unfortunately, it was mainly downhill from there. Ultimately, the club suffered a disastrous double relegation and, after a poor start to the 2014–15 season, Tranmere were relegated from the Football League on 25 April 2015, ending their 94-year stay in the league.

In 2014 it had been announced that former player and FA chief executive Mark Palios and his wife Nicola were taking a controlling interest in the club from outgoing chairman Johnson. They immediately proceeded to carry out stadium and pitch improvements.

After examining options about relocating, the owners announced that they were committed to keeping

Tranmere Rovers at Prenton Park for the foreseeable future and planned to redevelop the stadium to help the club generate revenue through non-footballing activities throughout the year. The project would be funded in part by the sale of the Ingleborough Road training pitches, close to Prenton Park, for housing.

In 2016 Rovers announced a two-year club partnership with North Star Environmental Ltd, which will see the Kop Stand renamed the North Star Environmental Kop.

Things look far better on the pitch too; Tranmere finished as runners-up in the Vanarama National League in 2016–17, but a return to the Football League was denied by defeat in the play-off final.

Address: Hillary Street, Walsall, Staffordshire WS2 9BZ

Highest attendance: 25,453 v Newcastle United, 29 August 1961

First league match: Walsall 2–0 v Burton Wanderers, 5 September 1896

Final league match: Walsall 1–1 v Rotherham United, 1 May 1990

Ground layout: Main Stand, Popular Terrace, Railway End/Laundry End, Hillary Street End

Status: Demolished

Current stadium: Bescot Stadium (Banks's Stadium)

Amalgamated from two previous town clubs, Walsall moved to Fellows Park in 1896, when it was originally known by its location as Hillary Street. Within four years the club found itself playing back at its former home on West Bromwich Road after rent difficulties before returning to Hillary Street for a barren 20-year period of non-league football. In 1930, nine years after the club's election to the Football League, the ground was renamed Fellows Park in honour of the chairman (H. L. Fellows) who had supported them during their years in the football doldrums.

The ground was all terraced for many years, though only on three sides as there was a brick wall running across one end of the ground, which formed the back of the adjacent Orgill's Laundry. The early 1930s saw the seated Main Stand constructed, though it only ran along part of the length of the pitch. This stand, which had a number of supporting pillars, had terracing to the front and one side of it. The seating in this stand was elevated above pitch level, which meant that supporters had to climb a small set of stairs to enter the seated area.

This was closely followed in 1933 by the installation of a rear roof with supporting pillars over the Popular Terrace, which stood opposite. The roof was hastily erected in anticipation of the forthcoming FA Cup tie against First Division aristocrats Arsenal. Third Division Walsall won 2–0 creating one of the biggest cup shocks of all time.

Floodlights were installed in 1957 and the first floodlit game to be played at Fellows Park was a friendly in the December of that year against Falkirk. In 1960 the laundry and associated brick wall were demolished and a small open terrace was constructed; this became known as the Railway End. New dressing rooms were installed following Walsall's return to the Second Division in 1961 after an absence of 60 years,

The Popular Terrace, 1970.

and on 29 August 1961, a record crowd of 25,453 packed into the ground to watch the Saddlers take on Newcastle United.

Four years later, a roof was constructed over the opposite terrace, the Hillary Street End. This terrace extended around two corners of the ground, one of which was covered. The Main Stand was extended in 1975 to accommodate over 1,000 more seated spectators, as well as partially covering the front paddock.

The ground was not known for its aesthetic qualities; the Hillary Street End roof was staggered in size, and the Main Stand, built in different stages, gave it a thrown together look. By the early 1980s Fellows Park was rapidly becoming unfit for purpose. In 1983, during the second leg of a League Cup semi-final against Liverpool, walls collapsed at both ends of the ground and 24 spectators were injured. Thankfully nobody was seriously hurt.

When the ground suffered through safety restrictions and had its capacity halved in 1985, thoughts quickly began to turn towards a new stadium. By 1988 plans had been approved, and within two years work began on the site of an old Severn Trent sewage works adjacent to the M6 at Bescot, just a quarter of a mile from Fellows Park.

The last three seasons at Fellows Park were certainly eventful; a promotion to Division Two was quickly followed by two bottom-placed finishes, ensuring Walsall bade farewell to their home in far from happy circumstances. Shortly after the final league game, Fellows Park was completely demolished and is now the site of a supermarket complex.

The new Bescot Stadium was ready for the 1990–91 season and a reminder of Fellows Park remained in the new stadium in the name of the H. L. Fellows Stand. From 1990 the club faced their future in the league's basement division and though they've fought their way back up to a level as high as the Championship, the club have spent the last decade firmly ensconced as a mid-table third-tier club.

Above: The open Railway End, 1989.

Below: The Main Stand, 1970s.

West Ham United

Upton Park

Address: Boleyn Ground, Green Street, Upton Park, London E13 9AZ

Highest attendance: 42,322 v Tottenham Hotspur, 17 October 1970

First league match: West Ham United 1-1 v Lincoln City, 30 August 1919

Final league match: West Ham United 3-2 v Manchester United, 10 May 2016

International matches: England (2003), England U-18, U-20, U-21, International friendlies

Ground-sharing: Charlton Athletic (1991–1992)

Other usages: Boxing

Ground layout: The Bobby Moore Stand, The Sir Trevor Brooking Stand, The Betway Stand, The East Stand

Status: Demolition in progress

Current stadium: London Stadium

Right: The old East Stand, 1966.

Opposite: Centenary Stand/Sir Trevor Brooking Stand, 2002.

When West Ham United, formed as Thames Ironworks in 1895, eventually left the spacious Memorial Ground at Canning Town in May 1904, their new home in Upton Park was originally a cabbage patch where a Catholic School and reformatory stood, just within the confines of East Ham. The Boleyn Ground took its name from the house which stood until the 1950s in Green Street next to the ground. It became known as the Boleyn Castle after Anne Boleyn, but this was not founded on fact, as the 'castle' was indeed merely a building known as Green Street House built in 1544, its only similarity to a castle being two distinctive castellated turrets. There is tenuous folklore that suggests Anne Boleyn had either stayed at or owned the house. The club rented Green Street House and grounds from the Catholic Church. Although many people refer to Upton Park as the name of the Hammers' ground, it is in fact the London district that the Boleyn Ground resides in.

Unlike the grander London football grounds, a master plan or blueprint for the development of the Boleyn Ground never really existed. Rather, it was allowed to evolve as circumstances demanded, though one of its lasting characteristics, the close proximity of the crowd to the pitch, was present from the start.

Knocked into some kind of shape in just seven weeks during the summer of 1904, the ground's principal feature was a long, low grandstand on the Green Street side, the first of four different West Stands to occupy that part of the ground over time. A changing shed was set in one corner, this being an odd-shaped elevated pavilion erected for the benefit of club directors and the press; the pitch was tightly enclosed by a wooden fence.

Having outgrown the first development, in 1913 a bigger West Stand was built, comprising an elevated seating deck and a large area of covered standing. At the same time, terraces that would later become the North and South Banks were raised at either end.

West Ham didn't join the Football League until 1919 when the competition was extended to 44 clubs, but as the club continued to gather support from the working-class population of the East End, it established its enduring identity as standard-bearers for east London. The Hammers quickly made an impression in the Second Division, winning promotion to the First Division in 1922–23, and also participating in the famous 'White Horse' FA Cup final, which was the first to be held at Wembley.

A ground more in keeping with their newly acquired First Division status was the next item on the agenda, and in 1925 West Ham's directors authorised a rebuilding programme costing £45,000. A towering double-decker grandstand rose up on the west Green Street side of the ground, seating 4,600, with room for a similar number of standing spectators in the section below the seating deck; the stand was easily the rival of any other in London at the time. The roof from the previous grandstand was salvaged and redeployed at the southern end, providing additional covered accommodation for 'shilling' spectators.

Also at this time a simple roof was added to the east side. Known as the Chicken Run, this rudimentary stand contained wooden terracing and had originally been open to the elements before the roof was added. It was surrounded by a sort of wire similar to that used on chicken runs and when viewed from the opposite side of the ground it looked indeed just like a chicken run.

By the time all the work was completed, capacity had increased from 32,000 to 45,000. Despite this, West Ham were relegated in 1932.

There is some confusion as to the Boleyn Ground's record attendance, for the club's records were lost during the Second World War. Modern reference books give the record as 42,322 against Tottenham in 1970, but pre-war crowds of 44,810 (v Birmingham City, FA Cup, 4 March 1933) and 43,528 (v Charlton Athletic, Second Division, 18 April 1936) are also sometimes quoted.

Due to its closeness to the docks, the Boleyn Ground found itself in the firing line during the Second World War, with the South Bank, Chicken Run and the club's offices all sustaining bomb damage in 1944 from a V-1 flying bomb. Though it took a while to effect repairs, with the club having to play its games away from home, in true 'make do and mend' fashion the Boleyn Ground was soon up and running again once football resumed after the war.

Although West Ham did not regain their First Division status until 1958, the club installed floodlights in 1953. The first match under lights took place on 16 April, when a crowd of 25,000 watched a friendly against First Division Tottenham Hotspur.

Following promotion to the First Division in 1958, which came after an absence of over 25 years, attention turned to improving the ground. The demolition of the remains of the dilapidated Boleyn Castle freed up space to make a new car park and a new entrance off Green Street.

Then in 1961 the North Bank gained a roof. Unlike the roof at the smaller South Bank, which only covered the rear portion of the terracing, the North Bank roof stretched down to encompass the whole of the terracing At the same time a new set of floodlights, a four-corner tower installation costing £15,000, was erected. In 1965 the lopsided appearance of the West Stand was finally addressed, when an extra bay was built, boosting capacity by a further 700.

It was during this time in the 1960s that West Ham really came into their own, being winners of the FA Cup in 1963–64, and the European Cup Winners' Cup in 1964–65. The year 1966 also figured large, with the club providing three members of England's World Cup winning team. The ground at which Bobby Moore, Geoff Hurst and Martin Peters paraded their skills was essentially a slightly updated version of the venue as developed in 1925.

Plans to replace the Chicken Run had first come to light in the 1930s, but somehow the structure tottered on until 1968. By that stage it was an ageing relic of

timber and rusting corrugated iron, not to mention a serious fire hazard. The club would have preferred to build a grandstand similar in dimensions to the West Stand, but due to a lack of space opted instead for a modest cantilever stand with 3,500 seats that was fully opened for the first time in January 1969. So as to maintain the tradition of the Chicken Run, a terrace holding 4,000, the same capacity as the old stand, was constructed in front of the seating deck. The development cost £170,000. Despite the later conversion to seats, West Ham fans still referred to this side of the ground as the Chicken Run.

The ground remained much the same until the early 1990s. The acquisition of extra land adjacent to Green Street in 1991 was a lifesaver, for it freed up space for expansion. Following the failure of a bond scheme, with only 800 taking up the offer, West Ham turned instead to the commercial banks to get the Boleyn Ground revamp underway.

For the 1991–92 season and part of the following season, Upton Park was also home to Charlton Athletic who played there following their exit from their ground-sharing arrangement with Crystal Palace at Selhurst Park, occasioned by Wimbledon moving into Selhurst when they left Plough Lane.

Upton Park's West Stand, 2002, newly built.

In 1993 the South Bank was replaced by a new 9,000-seat, two-tier stand named in honour of former captain Bobby Moore, who had died earlier that year. A handsome structure, which shared some of the same design features of Highbury's North Bank, the stand also incorporated executive boxes as well as a digital clock.

In 1995 the North Bank was replaced by a new 6,000-seat, two-tier stand named The Centenary Stand honouring the Hammers 100th season. It was renamed the Sir Trevor Brooking Stand in 2009. The East Stand Lower was also made all seater.

Finally in 2001 the West Stand was replaced by a new 15,000-seat, two-tier stand named The Doc Martens Stand. This incorporated executive boxes on two levels as well as the West Ham United Hotel. It was also the largest single football stand in London;

in fact it was so large that it was visible from the A406 North Circular Road and from the A13 Newham Way. It was opened by HM the Queen. For sponsorship reasons, this later became firstly The Alpari Stand and subsequently the Betway Stand.

The Taylor Report did however ask serious questions about the continued longer-term viability of the Boleyn Ground, with the venue's capacity falling to 29,000. Plans were drawn up to further develop the ground, but were put on hold after a combination of resistance from local residents on roads behind the stand and the club's relegation from the Premier League in 2003, which spiralled the club into debt. They were resurrected in 2005 following promotion. However, by 2006 rumours were rife about a move away from Upton Park.

Discussions soon turned to the use of the Olympic Stadium (after the 2012 games), though initial talks in 2007 broke down. On 23 March 2010 the club announced they were in fact working on a joint bid with Newham Borough Council to move into the Olympic Stadium. After a long and protracted bidding process that involved judicial reviews from rival bidders, and the deal collapsing at one point, on 22 March 2013 it was announced that the club's tenancy bid had been successful and that West Ham would take over a 99-year lease and re-locate there in August 2016.

When the Premier League fixtures were drawn up at the start of the 2015–16 season, Swansea City were planned to be West Ham's final opponents at the Boleyn Ground, on 7 May 2016. Manchester United had been scheduled to play their league match at the Boleyn on 23 April; however, because of their involvement in the FA Cup, the fixture was rearranged to 10 May 2016, and that became the final match. West Ham departed Upton Park on a winning note, 3–2.

By July 2016 the seats had been removed from the ground and it was boarded up and handed over to developers for demolition and redevelopment. Demolition of the ground commenced in earnest in September 2016. The task was due to take several months to complete. The John Lyall gates were to be retained and reinstalled at the Olympic Stadium.

Upton Park will become a housing development called Upton Gardens, consisting of luxury flats and affordable housing (over 800 dwellings in total). There are plans to incorporate a library, cycle routes, a crèche, community hall and retail outlets. Importantly, West Ham's rich history will be commemorated with a statue of Hammers legend and England's World Cup winning captain, Bobby Moore. The centre circle of the Boleyn Ground pitch will be preserved in a landscaped courtyard while the halfway line will be illuminated through the use of in-laid lighting.

The Hammers started the 2016–17 Premier League season at the renamed London Stadium, but experienced some teething troubles at the start, acclimatising to their spacious new home.

Wigan Athletic   Springfield Park

Address: Springfield Park, Wigan, Lancashire WN6 7BA

Highest attendance: 30,443 v Sheffield Wednesday (FA Cup), 12 January 1929

First league match: Wigan Athletic 0-3 v Grimsby Town, 23 August 1978

Final league match: Wigan Athletic 1-1 v Manchester City, 15 May 1999

Other usages: Rugby League, Cycling, Athletics, Blackburn Rovers Reserves

Ground layout: Main Stand/Phoenix Stand, Popular Side/St Andrews Stand, Shevington End, Town End

Status: Demolished

Current stadium: DW Stadium

Right: The old St Andrews Stand, 1969.

Springfield Park is best known for housing Wigan Athletic from their formation until 1999. It hosted league football from 1978, but the first time the stadium tasted league action was some 46 years earlier when Wigan Borough briefly graced the Third Division North from its inception in 1921 until 1932.

The ground was built and opened in 1897 costing £16,000 and in total played host to five separate association football clubs bearing the Wigan name, but Athletic were undoubtedly the most successful. They began their tenure in the wake of Borough's demise in 1932. After lengthy negotiations, Wigan Athletic purchased the ground from the owner of the Woodhouse Lane dog track for £2,800 with the proviso that greyhound racing never took place there.

The facilities at the ground improved markedly in the decade or so that Wigan Borough played league football at Springfield Park. In the early 1920s a new main stand was constructed, which was 95 yards long fronted by a paddock which was partially covered; the stand seated 2,000 people. Roofing cover was provided at the Shevington End. Also the Popular Side Stand (later to be the St Andrews Stand) was built extending from the halfway line down towards the Shevington End. There was shelter on the Popular Side for 5,000, and there were plans to extend the shelter to cover a further 3,000.

In 1929 Wigan Borough drew the current Football League champions, Sheffield Wednesday, in the FA Cup. On the day of the match, 12 January, the gates were opened at 12 o'clock and the official record attendance was given as 30,443.

During the six years of the Second World War, Springfield Park was maintained by the 'older

directors', but despite their best efforts the Grandstand needed significant repair work and the Popular Side shelter required a new roof after the hostilities. At this time 500 of the 2,000 seats in the grandstand were upholstered. In the post-war years, Wigan played in the Cheshire County League and the Lancashire Combination.

On 30 May 1953 the Main Stand was razed to the ground by fire, resulting in major fundraising efforts for the construction of a new stand. The following season, a large crowd saw the Main Stand (also known as the Phoenix Stand) opened but still not fully complete, and 27,526 watched Wigan Athletic beat Hereford United 4–1 in the FA Cup. To the present day, it is considered the largest-ever attendance recorded between two non-league clubs at a non-league ground (excluding Wembley finals). The

construction of the middle section of the new stand was completed for the start of the 1954–55 season. The stand cost £23,000 and provided seats for 2,000 spectators.

The planned end sections which would have extended the new stand along the whole length of the pitch were never built in the following years due to a lack of funds.

The stadium was completed by the Town and Shevington Ends behind the goals. Both had a semi-circular nature that could be seen at the front of the terraces, as at one time there was a cycle track around the playing area. The Town End was an open terrace.

The latter, also known colloquially as 'the grassy bank', was endowed with a rather unusual grass verge at the top of its banking, where spectators could stand. However, after new safety regulations in the

early 1990s a fence was put in place at the rear of the terrace to prevent fans standing there.

Floodlights made their appearance on 19 October 1965 for a Northern Floodlit League match against Crewe Alexandra, although the official unveiling took place five days later for a friendly against Manchester City, which saw 10,119 attend. This was many years before floodlights were installed at the rugby league ground at Central Park. Three years later, Wigan became founder members of the Northern Premier League.

In October 1973 Wigan Athletic announced that a new stand was to be erected on the Shevington End at a cost of £45,000, with work commencing in a few months' time. It was hoped that on completion of the project the seating capacity would be 1,337, but as finances were limited, the building work would start with a 90ft centre section providing cover for standing spectators. The steelwork from the present stand was to be used as a basis for bar and canteen facilities.

The work was part funded by brewers, Greenall Whitley. The stand, which was never finished, was demolished in 1976 and the steelwork was sold to a local engineering firm for a profit, this due to a steel shortage at the time. Officially, the stand was removed because it stood too close to the pitch and impaired visibility and a new, smaller stand was constructed as a replacement.

League football continued to elude the team until 1978, many considering that the club were being punished for prior failings in the town's attempts to firmly establish a stable football club. During this period, Wigan Athletic carved itself out as a giant in non-league circles and also forged a reputation as a famous FA Cup giant killer. They were finally elected, at the 34th attempt, at the expense of neighbours Southport.

Election to the Football League brought numerous small improvements to the ground, much work being completed by volunteers. Within two years, new seats had been fitted throughout the Phoenix Stand, and terracing had been built in front of the main stand. The floodlight modernisation was also completed as fittings and bulbs from the original system had become obsolete. The new equipment would allow for televised floodlit matches. It was calculated that in those two years, £100,000 had been spent on ground improvements.

Work was then started on the extra terracing behind the Town End goal and although work was halted by a long and hard winter, the project was completed for the start of the 1980–81 season.

In February 1986 the new chairman wasted no time unveiling sensational plans to turn Springfield Park into a £2.5 million super stadium with a 15,000 all-seater sports arena. The scheme did not get past the design stage. Instead, the St Andrews Stand was rebuilt in the summer of 1987, replacing the old dog-legged stand that was a combination of two previous endeavours, one from the early 1920s and an extension from the late 1950s. The new covered section ran along the full length of the pitch and housed a refreshment bar.

In March 1990 a second attempt to convert Springfield Park into an all-seater stadium was unveiled. The scheme would cost £3 million, house between 12,000 to 15,000 fans and would involve moving the pitch away from St Andrews Drive resulting in the demolition of the Phoenix Stand. This proposal also failed to get past the planning stage. The ground fell into disrepair in the early 1990s and with the football team struggling, large parts of the ground were sectioned off by the local council.

On 18 December 1992, exactly seven years after he took control, the chairman sold Wigan Athletic to Corporate Resources Limited, headed by Stephen Gage and Nick Bitel. During the close season in 1994, the St Andrews Terrace was re-roofed and new crush barriers installed. These were bought from Villa Park after their Holte End had been re-developed. After seeing his repeated attempts to relocate the Latics to

the Robin Park athletics ground scuppered by Wigan Council, Stephen Gage finally admitted defeat when he sold the Latics and Springfield Park to sports-shop mogul Dave Whelan on 27 February 1995 for around £1 million. Whelan immediately started to improve the facilities at Springfield Park.

Only one trophy was lifted at Springfield Park in its entire history, secured when Athletic beat Mansfield Town 2–0 to lift the Third Division title in 1997 in a dramatic last-day tussle with Fulham.

On 9 September 1998 Springfield Park had new owners as the ground was sold to developers for an undisclosed fee. The firm was to build a housing development of 100 three- or four-bedroom dwellings at the site on completion of the new stadium. After the last match in May, the ground, stand and pitch were badly damaged by vandals overnight, forcing staff into temporary accommodation. Soon after, vandals broke into the souvenir shop and started a fire which destroyed the Phoenix stand and effectively put an end to any further use of Springfield Park.

Demolition work started on 14 June 1999 for safety reasons, due to the condition of the ground, and by the middle of July the stadium was reduced to rubble. The only token nod to Wigan's former home at the new housing development being the name of one of the main roads, Lyon Road, named after the legendary non-league Wigan goal machine Harry Lyon.

Wigan moved to the £30 million purpose-built 25,000-seater stadium named after the chairman's shop chain, the JJB Stadium. This became the DW Stadium in 2009. True to Whelan's 10-year promise, Wigan went on to reach the Premier League in 2005, and spent eight years in the top flight, before becoming in 2013 the first team ever to win the FA Cup and be relegated in the same season. Since then they suffered relegation to League One, but bounced back almost immediately. Sadly, they could not consolidate, and were once again relegated from the Championship at the end of the 2016–17 season.

Top: Springfield Park's East/Main Stand, 1969.

Above: Town End, 1990.

Opposite: Shevington End, with the unfinished stand.

Wimbledon

Address: Plough Lane, Wimbledon, London SW19

Highest attendance: 18,080 v HMS Victory (FA Amateur Cup), 2 March 1935

First league match: Wimbledon 3-3 v Halifax, 20 August 1977

Final league match: Wimbledon 0-3 v Crystal Palace, 4 May 1991

International matches: England amateur

Other usages: Crystal Palace Reserves

Ground layout: Main Stand, South Stand, Durnsford Road End, Wandle End

Status: Demolished

Current stadium: Stadium mk (as MK Dons)

Plough Lane, built on disused swampland joining Haydon Road, was the home of the fabled Wimbledon, the underdog club that enjoyed a meteoric rise up the Football League and into the nation's heart. Leaving too soon, things were never the same for the club that controversially relocated and changed name in 2003, effectively ending any association with history.

Initially formed as Wimbledon Old Central after a school, they changed their name in 1905. Re-formed as Wimbledon Borough, the club had played on Wimbledon Common before arriving at Plough Lane in 1912. Though they were a very successful and popular amateur side, it would be another 64 years before they achieved Football League status.

On arrival, the pitch was fenced in and the playing surface improved, while a dressing room was built. A stand holding 500 spectators was erected, and Wimbledon played their first match at the ground on 7 September 1912. Improvements continued to be made to the ground during the First World War, and the ground soon became the pride of the club.

Eleven years after arriving, the club purchased the stand from Clapton (now Leyton) Orient, which they deposited on the south side of the stadium. The terrace in front of the North Stand was improved during 1932–33. The South Stand was bombed during the Second World War but was fully restored in time for the 1950–51 season and glass panels were placed on the ends of both stands. Floodlights were purchased in 1954 and finally the Main Stand was completely replaced in 1957.

Two years after that the ground's freehold was purchased, with a pre-emption clause, from Merton Borough Council by the chairman for £8,250 who then donated the ground to the club, and the lights purchased five years earlier were finally erected at a cost of £4,000. The first match under the new floodlights took place on 3 October 1960, a London Charity Cup match against Arsenal.

Also in that year, a small cantilever roof over part of the terracing at the Durnsford Road End where the home fans gathered was constructed. The Wandle End would remain open to the elements. The terracing was also concreted. Following this surge, only basic maintenance was later done.

Following successes at amateur level, the decision was taken to turn professional for the 1964–65 season and to enter the Southern League. Wimbledon had continued success in their new league, finishing as runners-up at the first attempt. Wimbledon became nationally famous during an FA Cup run in the 1974–75 season, defeating Burnley at Turf Moor and then holding reigning First Division champions Leeds United to a 0–0 draw at Elland Road.

After winning the Southern League three seasons running from 1974–75, Wimbledon were elected to the Football League in place of Workington. The

South Stand, 1969.

Durnsford Road End, 1989.

Right: Main Stand, 1969.

ground remained largely unchanged, and even after election, little money was spent on improvements.

Despite this promotion to league status, Wimbledon still had financial troubles. To try to ease the strain, the club had bought out the pre-emption clause inserted back in 1959 for £100,000 in April 1983, and a year later, sold the ground to businessman Sam Hammam for £3 million.

The club soared from the Fourth Division to the First in just four years, after briefly yo-yoing between the Third and Fourth. Even after elevation to the top flight, apart from some new crush barriers, tweaks to the turnstiles, some seats and the obligatory coat of paint, the ground remained largely as it had been in its amateur days. The side's rise culminated in the famous 1988 1–0 FA Cup final victory over Liverpool at Wembley.

Plans to build a new 20,000 all-seater stadium in the London Borough of Merton had been announced and approved by the local council soon after the FA Cup win, but the stadium was never built and a public park was later erected on its planned site.

The Taylor Report recommendations forced Wimbledon to consider their future and, deciding redevelopment would be too costly, they announced a ground share with Crystal Palace, beginning in the 1991–92 season. Many of the Wimbledon faithful consider that the decision was made in haste and that the site could have been re-developed, albeit with difficulty. The reserve sides of both those clubs would continue to play at Plough Lane until 1998.

Three years later in 1995 chairman Sam Hamman sold Plough Lane to a supermarket chain, who attempted unsuccessfully to build a store on the site. The site decayed into dereliction over the years that negotiations took place. Plough Lane was finally sold on to housing developers in 2002. The ground was demolished later that year and became a private housing estate known as Reynolds Gate, completed in 2008. The blocks of the 570 flats fittingly bear the names of former footballing heroes.

Wimbledon would eventually extend their 'temporary' stay at Selhurst Park to 12 long years until the club's relocation to Milton Keynes in 2003. At the end of their first season in Milton Keynes, Wimbledon were relegated to the third tier. The team were re-branded in 2004 as the MK Dons. Plough Lane was where it all went right for Wimbledon, and many think more of an effort could and should have been made to stay there. Instead the stadium – and also the club – was eventually lost.

MK Dons spent three years at the converted National Hockey Stadium, before relocating again to the purpose-built Stadium mk in 2007. They have gone on to briefly achieve Championship status, but are currently competing in League One.

AFC Wimbledon, their spiritual successors founded by disaffected supporters, play in Kingston at Kingsmeadow, having purchased the ground, with Kingstonian becoming ground-sharing tenants. When AFC Wimbledon was formed, it affiliated to both the London and Surrey Football Associations, and entered the Premier Division of the Combined Counties League, the ninth tier in English football. In its short history the club has been extremely successful, being promoted six times in thirteen seasons, going up from that ninth tier (Combined Counties Premier) to League One, where they currently reside.

Plans to build a new 20,000 all-seater stadium for AFC Wimbledon on the nearby site of the Wimbledon greyhound track, approximately 200 yards from the original Plough Lane stadium, were approved by Merton Council in 2016. Season 2016–17 saw the first-ever league encounter between the MK Dons and AFC Wimbledon.

National Hockey Stadium – see page 159.

Workington

Address: Borough Park, Workington, Cumbria CA14 2DT

Highest attendance: 21,000 v Manchester United (FA Cup), 4 January 1958

First league match: Workington 3-1 v Chesterfield, 22 August 1951

Final league match: Workington 0-1 v Newport County, 14 May 1977

Other usages: Rugby League

Ground layout: Main Stand, Popular Side, Town End, Derwent End

Status: Extant

Current stadium: Borough Park

Right: Popular Side, 1960s.

Below: Derwent End, 1987.

Borough Park is a stadium highly coveted by its tenants – Workington AFC. They took up residence in 1937, a previous incarnation of the club having played at the Lonsdale Park dog track before dissolving in 1911. This original Workington AFC had been one of the founder members of the Cumberland Association League in 1890. This stadium was built, with the assistance of the council, on a refuse dump that was regarded as waste ground with no value. A Workington club re-formed in 1921, playing in the North Eastern League.

A Main Stand on the west side, capable of seating 1,000 fans, was built when the club moved in, and included dressing rooms and offices. The remainder of the stadium was banking. Borough Park was also the home of the town's rugby league club Workington Town from when they formed just after the Second World War until they moved out in 1956 to their own ground, nearby Derwent Park.

Workington set about securing election to the Football League, and this was achieved in 1951 when the club were voted into the Third Division North, replacing New Brighton and, against the odds, Borough Park would go on to play host to some of the country's elite. On this promotion, the

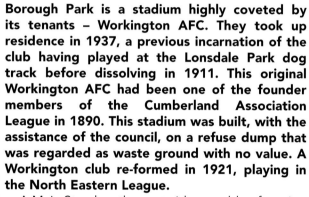

Main Stand, 1970s.

Town End, 1987.

embankments were converted to terracing, and two more stands were erected in the north-west and south-west corners of the ground.

The ground underwent further expansion during the 1950s as the Main Stand was extended to hold 2,000 and the terracing on the eastern side of the pitch was roofed in 1956. Initial struggles in the Third Division North did not bode well and the club dropped to the Fourth Division on the FA's re-shuffling of the league in 1958. In that 1957–58 season they played the Manchester United team known as the Busby Babes at Borough Park in the third round of the FA Cup, attracting a record crowd of 21,000. United won 3–1, but just a month later half the United side perished in the snow at Munich.

A brief period of success in the 1960s saw not only promotion to the Third Division but a period in which Workington reached League Cup quarter-finals in consecutive seasons as they tangled with West Ham and Chelsea, the latter unable to secure victory when they visited Borough Park.

A very near miss on promotion to the Second Division preceded a drop back to the Fourth in 1967.

In 1967–68 they held First Division Fulham to a draw in the League Cup, being wrongly denied a last-minute winning goal.

Workington would remain basement-dwellers for a decade before being voted out of the Football League in 1977 in favour of up-and-coming Wimbledon. In their final season, Workington won just four league games and conceded over 100 league goals.

The intervening years have made the stadium look worn. The Main Stand became a casualty of health and safety regulations following the 1985 fire at Bradford, and as a result was partially dismantled at a later date; the roof and seating were crudely removed, leaving just the changing rooms, offices and restaurant. It created an ugly, heavily slanted, unfinished-looking building on the west side. This was renovated later with an attractive red roof added. Later, the original floodlight pylons in each corner were cut down to size for safety reasons. Opposite remains the Popular Side, where the stadium's 500 seats are located. Left of that is the Town End, which is 75 per cent covered by a corrugated tin roof running round towards the Main Stand; the amount of rust visible among its

girders suggest that this structure won't survive the salty sea air much longer.

Directly opposite is the Derwent, or River End, a once-covered goal-side terrace with a few terrace steps remaining in use, the rest being abandoned as a grassy bank at the top. Despite plans for a shared stadium at the adjacent Derwent Park with rugby league neighbours Workington Town, the football club have remained determined to hang on to their dilapidated home, even though the council would have developed a new stadium for the club from the resulting windfall of selling the area for retail development.

After many years lost in the soccer wilderness, Workington fought their way back, leaving them at one stage just two promotions away from a return to the Football League. The stadium received a two-year facelift to meet FA ground regulations. However, their fortunes have since ebbed away again and the club currently plies its trade at level seven of the pyramid, the Northern Premier League, Premier Division.

Wrexham

Racecourse Ground

Address: Mold Road, Wrexham, Clwyd, North Wales LL11 2AH

Highest attendance: 34,445 v Manchester United, (FA Cup), 26 January 1957

First league match: Wrexham 0-2 v Hartlepool United, 27 August 1921

Final league match: Wrexham 1-3 v Accrington Stanley, 26 April 2008

International matches: Wales (Football), Wales (Rugby Union), Wales (Rugby League)

Ground-sharing: North Wales Crusaders

Other usages: Rugby League, Rugby Union, Cricket, Horse Racing, Rock Concerts, Liverpool/Liverpool Reserves, Bangor City, Cefn Druids

Ground layout: Yale Stand, Mold Road Stand, Town End/Kop, Glyndwr University Stand

Status: Extant

Current stadium: Racecourse Ground (Glyndwr University Racecourse Stadium)

Right: The old Mold Road Stand, 1980.

Opposite top: The old Mold Road Stand, 1980s.

Opposite bottom: Glyndwr University Stand, 2002.

Wrexham's Racecourse Ground may no longer house league football, but its rich history speaks for itself; it is the oldest venue in the world still open to have hosted international football.

Wrexham Football Club have played at the Racecourse Ground since being formed in the local Turf Hotel public house in October 1864. However, Wrexham played their home games at the Recreation Ground in Rhosddu from 1881 to 1883, due to the increase in the rent demanded from the owners, Wrexham Cricket Club. Before the club was formed, the ground was mainly used for cricket and occasionally horse racing, hence the name. After several unsuccessful attempts, Wrexham were finally elected to the Birmingham and District League for the 1905–06 season.

During their time in the Birmingham and District League, Wrexham won the Welsh Cup six times. They also reached the First Round proper of the FA Cup for a second time in the 1908–09 season before losing a replay to Exeter City.

It was when Wrexham were elected to the Football League Third Division North in 1921 that work on the Racecourse Ground really began to pick up; the open terracing behind the goal opposite the famed Kop End was covered thanks to the supporters' club's funds, and a stand was constructed on the Mold Road side.

It was after the Second World War that the Crispin Lane End or Town End Kop began to take shape, the supporters themselves laying down the concrete terracing in 1952 for what would become, at the time, the largest terrace in the league, holding 4,000 spectators. Five years later, the largest-ever attendance at the Racecourse was set when 34,445 people gathered to witness an FA Cup fourth round tie against Manchester United. On 30 September 1959 the Racecourse saw the switching on of the newly installed floodlights for a match against Swindon Town.

After promotion in 1962 the club erected a small stand on the Kop terrace, bizarrely taken from the frame of a nearby cinema. Providing cover for 1,000, it became

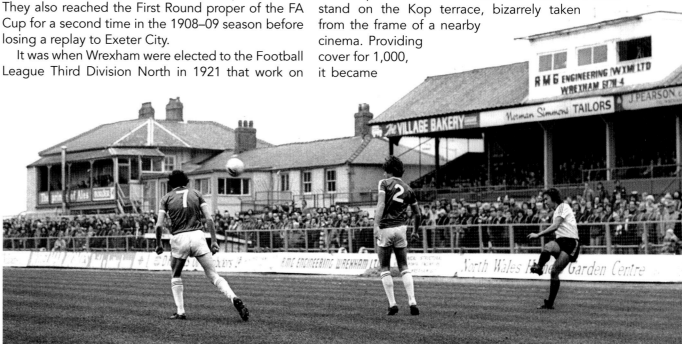

known as the 'pigeon loft' and lasted just 16 years before it was deemed unsafe; incredibly the stand was later sold on to Wrexham Rugby Club after being dismantled.

Regular European football, through the Welsh Cup, saw an increase in revenue which was re-invested in the ground. 1972 saw the Yale Stand constructed, named after the college situated behind it. It provided new dressing rooms, club offices and entertainment suites. It was a two-tiered stand which originally had terracing at the front, but was eventually converted to an all-seater facility. Wrexham reached the quarter-finals of the Cup Winners Cup in 1975–76 and also gained promotion to the Second Division in 1978.

In this year the Border Stand, taking its name from the owners Border Breweries, was erected opposite the Kop. The two-tier 2,800 capacity structure was again all seater, but originally had terracing at the front. The stand has possessed many names, but is currently known as the Glyndwr University Stand. In 1980 the Kop finally received adequate cover.

Despite not being the side of a decade previously, Wrexham still had the capability of providing a shock, as they showed in 1992, when as a Fourth Division side they knocked league champions Arsenal out of the FA Cup 2–1 at the Racecourse.

At this time the ground also held four rugby union internationals. Three of them were Wales friendlies against Romania. It also hosted a 1999 Rugby Union World Cup match between Japan and Samoa on 3 October 1999.

The latest modification to the stadium occurred in 1999 with the unveiling of the new Mold Road Stand, a state-of-the-art grandstand with a modern cantilevered roof built in three sections. The impressive new structure, originally named the Pryce Griffiths Stand after the then chairman (but since renamed the Mold Road Stand after the chairman sold the club to Alex Hamilton), has a capacity of 3,500 and also contains hospitality and conferencing facilities.

On 26 June 2002 the freehold to the Racecourse Ground was acquired by Wrexham AFC from Wolverhampton & Dudley Breweries for the sum of £300,000. On the same day, the ownership of the freehold was transferred by chairman Hamilton from Wrexham AFC to another of his companies. After this controversial change in ownership, the 125-year lease on the Racecourse held by Wrexham FC was renegotiated.

The new lease stated that the company could evict Wrexham FC from the Racecourse Ground upon 12 months' notice and payment of £1 million. The new lease also saw the club's annual rent increase significantly. In 2004 Wrexham were given a year's notice to quit the ground; this triggered a furious reaction from fans, and in a legal case running through to March 2006 the High Court ruled that the ownership of the freehold of the ground had been improperly transferred, and ownership reverted to the club's then-administrators (the club having gone into administration in December 2004 with debts of £2.6 million).

Wrexham became the first league club to suffer a 10-point deduction under the new rule for being placed in administration, dropping them from the middle of the League One table to the relegation zone, and this subsequently condemned Wrexham to relegation.

With the club's emergence from administration in May 2006, ownership of the ground passed to a new company, Wrexham Football Club (2006) Ltd, owned by Geoff Moss and Ian Roberts. They passed ownership of the football ground to a new holding company Wrexham Village Ltd.

In 2008 Wrexham Village proposed a joint venture development with a third party, to develop a student village area near the site of the Kop stand. The £40 million project would be developed in conjunction with Glyndwr University to house over 800 students, and take place in two phases. However, due to the global recession, the company found it hard to find a

development partner, and the land and project was eventually sold freehold in 2009 to another company owned by Moss and Roberts.

The stadium looked better than it had in years but events on the pitch weren't going so well as Wrexham were relegated from the Football League in 2008. The Racecourse Ground had gone from an international venue that raised some eyebrows, to

one equipped for such an occasion, yet without a league team inhabiting it. The ground also became home to rugby league with former European Super League club Crusaders arriving in 2010 after their departure from Bridgend. In 2011 Crusaders withdrew their Super League licence application and ultimately folded citing financial invalidity. However, a new club was formed – the North Wales Crusaders – who currently play in the Co-operative Championship One competition.

In August 2011, after a period of instability at Wrexham Village Ltd, the owning company of the stadium and both the football and rugby league clubs agreed to sell the stadium and associated training grounds to Glyndwr University. The proposed deal would allow both football and rugby teams to continue using the facilities. The purchase of the ground also resulted in the re-branding of the stadium, incorporating the university's name.

On 19 May 2014 work commenced at the Racecourse, providing a new pitch and sprinkler system and changing rooms for players and officials. The phase would also see better floodlighting and removal of cambers at the Kop end of the ground.

In another twist, in 2016 Wrexham Supporters Trust members voted overwhelmingly (99%) for the fan-owned club to take over the running of the stadium on a 99-year lease, but the fans and activities would need to make good a £200,000 shortfall.

Despite the dramatic events off the pitch, Wrexham still remain a non-league side although they have reached the play-offs on three consecutive occasions. They continue in a comfortable position in the Vanarama National League but a return to the Football League does not seem imminent.

Above left: The new Mold Road Stand, 2002.

Left: The Racecourse Ground's Yale Stand, 2002.

Wycombe Wanderers   Loakes Park

Address: Queen Alexandra Road, High Wycombe, Buckinghamshire HP11 2TT

Highest attendance: 15,850 v St Albans City (FA Amateur Cup), 25 February 1950

Ground layout: Main Stand, Cowshed Side, Hospital End, Gasworks End

Status: Demolished

Current stadium: Adams Park

Right: Loakes Park, after closure. The gates were transferred to Adams Park.

Below: Hospital End, 1989.

Loakes Park became the home of Wycombe Wanderers when their previous ground, Spring Meadow, was sold and built over by the London Marylebone railway line. An approach was made to Lord Carrington, who owned Wycombe Abbey and the surrounding estate which included Loakes Park, for permission to play football there. Permission was granted, with the first match taking place on Saturday 7 September 1895 against Park Grove.

The ground was located next to Wycombe General Hospital in the centre of the town and was later donated to the club by Frank Adams, a former Wanderers player who had bought the freehold on the ground from Lord Carrington in 1945.

In the summer of 1899 the club vacated Loakes Park temporarily to allow for the infamous bent pitch to be straightened. They played at various venues before returning for the 1901–02 season. The pitch would continue to have an enormous side-to-side drop, an estimate being 11 feet, during its lifetime. The summer of 1903 saw Loakes Park improved with a fund initiated to build a stand. This first stand was completed in January 1904.

Loakes Park was used for training artillerymen during the First World War and the club ceased to be active for its duration. In 1923 the stand at Loakes Park was redeveloped, including new changing rooms, at a cost of £1,500. Up to this time, the amateur club had played in various leagues before settling in the Isthmian League.

The 1930s started with the culmination of a dream as the club won the FA Amateur Cup for the only time in its history. Wycombe met Hayes in the final at Highbury on 11 April 1931. A crowd of 32,489 watched a tight competitive game that was decided by a single goal with just five minutes remaining. The profits from the cup run were used to build a corrugated cover, affectionately known as the Cowshed, along the length of the lower side of

Loakes Park's Main Stand, 1989. This was the final season at the ground.

Loakes Park. It was said that Wycombe Wanderers became the first amateur club to have stands on opposite sides of the ground.

The two ends of the ground, the Gasworks End and the Hospital End, would remain as uncovered terracing throughout the ground's lifetime.

On 19 April 1947, before an Isthmian League game at Loakes Park, Frank Adams presented the deeds to the club president. This single altruistic act, protected by trustees, secured the future of the club and paved the way for the successes that followed.

On 25 September 1963 the match between Wycombe Wanderers and Enfield saw floodlights used for the first time at Loakes Park. There were also significant changes off the pitch during that season. The chairman had concluded that Loakes Park would not pass a ground inspection if the club were ever

to seek promotion to the Football League and that there wasn't sufficient space or funding available to redevelop the ground. This sowed the seeds for an eventual move.

The trustees' role had been a mainly passive one until 1968 when the Health Authority sought initial discussions with the club for the expansion of Wycombe Hospital. Two years later, a consultative document showing plans of the extension over the whole of Loakes Park was produced. However, there were considerable difficulties in identifying suitable alternative sites for the club.

Wycombe became a real non-league force and in January 1975 arguably the most memorable match to be played at Loakes Park occurred in the third round of the FA Cup. At the time, Middlesbrough were near the top of the First Division and Wycombe

held them to a 0–0 draw. The game was watched by 12,000 people.

The decade that followed was difficult following the FA's decision to abolish amateur status, and Wycombe turned down opportunities to turn professional. However, dwindling attendances forced a re-think and they eventually joined a Conference forerunner in 1985.

Eventually a compulsory purchase order was placed on Loakes Park in the 1980s. However, Wycombe Wanderers had difficulties obtaining planning permission elsewhere, and nine alternative proposals at various locations in High Wycombe were all dismissed by the local planning authority. Only after the Home Secretary had intervened and overturned the initial rejection of a proposed ground at the end of Hillbottom Road could Wycombe Wanderers begin work on their new ground in 1989.

The summer of 1990 was an emotional and significant one. After 95 years at Loakes Park, the club moved to their new ground at Adams Park. Loakes Park had become a real home of which everyone had become extremely fond. The new ground was named after Frank Adams, an appropriate gesture to the benefactor who helped make it a reality.

The sale of Loakes Park would also provide a financial platform capable of funding a rise to the Football League. Three years later, the Chairboys achieved that promotion.

The site of Loakes Park was redeveloped, partly as extra car parking for the nearby hospital, and partly as new housing. Apart from a fence, no reminders of the old ground remain. The original gates from Loakes Park were transferred to the new stadium.

Almost 25 unbroken years later, Wycombe remain in the Football League and have spent their time in the two lowest tiers, but the team have produced some decent FA Cup and League Cup runs and shocks along the way.

Yeovil Town
Huish Athletic Ground

Highest attendance: 17,123 v Sunderland (FA Cup), 29 January 1949

Ground layout: Main Stand, North Terrace, Queen Street End, Brutton's End

Status: Demolished

Current stadium: Huish Park

Right: Queen Street End, 1990.

Yeovil Casuals first made an approach for the Huish field, then owned by a brewery, at the end of the 1897–98 season, but this was unsuccessful; negotiations, with the club now known as Yeovil Town, continued up to the start of the First World War, at which time the team merged with local rivals Petters United. The club were then playing at a ground adjacent to the Great Western Railway Yeovil Pen Mill railway station.

The summer of 1920 saw Yeovil & Petters United finally leave the Pen Mill Athletic Ground, after purchasing the land at Huish from the brewery. The name for the ground was borrowed from the name of a suburb in the town, Huish from the Old English hiwisc meaning a group of houses or a household.

The Huish Athletic Ground was more commonly referred to as Huish. Initially the terraces were flat with the only covered accommodation being in the form of a 300-seater main stand that had been brought from Pen Mill. That stand was soon extended at a cost of £733 to include dressing rooms and baths, and the structure remained in place until 1963.

Yeovil joined the Southern League in 1922. During the summer of the following year, 750 loads of earth were brought to the ground to form a terrace at the Queen Street End of the ground and the pitch was lengthened by four yards. In October and November a further 100 tons of materials were given by Westlands and hauled to the ground, and the club simultaneously opened negotiations with the Southern Railway to purchase 1,000 railway sleepers, at a cost of £50, to add steps to the terraces.

In 1924 the Supporters' Club was formed and three tea huts were purchased and installed at Huish.

During a good FA Cup run, additional terracing was added at the Brutton's End and toilets were installed. In November 1926 covered accommodation over the terraces at the Queen Street End was opened.

In 1931 the club purchased the freehold of further land from the brewery at the Brutton's End of the ground to increase accommodation. The next development of Huish came in the 1934–35 season when Yeovil reached the third round of the FA Cup for the first time and were drawn against Liverpool. In the two weeks between the time of the draw and the game being played, a small stand to hold 100 people and costing £250 was built in the corner at the Queen Street End. The stand acted as the directors' box and boardroom until the new main stand was built, and remained in place until 1983.

At a board meeting in February 1938 the first of many plans to level the Huish pitch was discussed, but the practicality and the cost of such a scheme made this impossible. The ground's slope became infamous, with the pitch sloping six feet along the halfway line and eight feet from corner to corner.

In January 1939, during a FA Cup third-round replay against Sheffield Wednesday, the game saw a new record crowd of 14,329 pack into Huish and the weight of the hordes of supporters who had climbed on to the roof of the Queen Street End had caused the roof to split from one end to the other; thankfully the spectators were safely removed. During the war, Huish was at first used by the War Office as an ammunitions store and then by the United States Army. In 1946–47 Alec Stock was appointed player/manager and the club's name reverted back to Yeovil Town.

The ground's most famous moment came four years after the war, when Huish hosted Yeovil's greatest giant-killing when the then non-league team defeated First Division side Sunderland in the fourth round of the FA Cup. A total of 17,123 spectators crammed into the ground, the largest ever attendance at Huish. The final score, a 2–1 Yeovil win, shocked the whole football world. It earned a tie with Manchester United.

On the back of that cup run, an extensive five-year ground improvement scheme was then put into operation. During this period the top bank of clinkers, earth and railway sleepers was removed and concrete terracing was installed. This work continued at the Brutton's End. The covering at the Queen Street End was removed and that terrace was then concreted. The final part of this project was to cover the North Terrace.

The cost of these extensive works was in excess of £5,000, and to provide this money an appeal was made to the traders of the town and a special fund, known as the Ground Development Fund, was instituted.

In 1954 a wall was built in front of the North Terrace and floodlights were installed at the ground. The first match under lights was a friendly game against Tottenham Hotspur, and the first competitive game under lights was against Bath City on 23 March 1955. In 1956 further work on the North Terrace was completed when the back of the stand was closed in.

The next major development of Huish took place in the summer of 1963 when the new stand was built, as the original Pen Mill main stand was demolished. Plans were drawn up and in March 1963 work commenced

Huish Athletic Ground's North Terrace, 1990, the final year.

when first a tea hut and then the old stand were demolished. By the first week in May, building work was underway, and at the start of the 1963–64 season the dressing rooms had been completed and the stand was open but the rest of the facilities were still under construction.

The new 2,000-seater Main Stand was finally completed just in time for an FA Cup tie with Crystal Palace on 7 December 1963, when the Social Club was opened. The new stand, which had cost £60,000 to build, gave the club new dressing rooms, plus an upstairs boardroom and a long bar which provided many community facilities, making the venue one of the hubs of the town.

At the start of the 1970s, scenes reminiscent of 1949 against Sunderland returned once again to Huish when Yeovil were drawn at home to Arsenal in the FA Cup. Admission charges were substantially raised. A wall was built in front of the Main Stand forming an enclosure to accommodate part of the 14,500 crowd. After a postponement, the game was played the following Wednesday afternoon, Arsenal winning 3–0.

At a board meeting held in November 1972 the directors once again discussed the possibility of levelling the Huish pitch; the cost would have been in the region of £17,000. The following month the club received an initial offer of £260,000 for the purchase of Huish.

The last decade of the ground saw the club spend over £200,000 in the interest of crowd safety. The main stand underwent major surgery with the introduction of staircases and fire proofing, and the terraces saw the introduction of crush barriers and segregation areas. In 1980 Yeovil were promoted to the forerunner of the Conference.

The slope that the club had refused to level during and after the war was, by the 1980s, one of the principal barriers to further promotion to the Football League. Furthermore, the Main stand was starting to develop rust in its supports that gave the club the

dilemma of whether to pay the high maintenance costs of keeping Huish alive or to sell up and move to another site. Further safety restrictions had reduced the official ground capacity to around 10,000 in its later years.

In March 1985 negotiations began with developers with a view to selling Huish and moving to a new stadium at Houndstone. At that stage a figure of £680,000 was placed upon Huish, which, over several years of negotiation, rose to a final figure of £2.8 million. In March 1989 the club finally got planning permission for an out-of-town stadium, on land previously used by the Houndstone Army Camp. Just over a year later a home match against Telford United on 5 May 1990 marked the end of 70 years of football at Huish.

The bulldozers moved in, and what was Huish football ground became a retail hypermarket, and Yeovil Town moved out to Houndstone, a £3.5 million stadium with the old ground's name partially surviving

in its Huish Park title. Most of the old ground ended up as rubble, and nothing of its past survives.

Yeovil's new ground provided a platform for success and the Glovers won promotion to the Football League in 2003. Since then, they have been promoted to as high as the Championship. A recent dip in fortunes however has seen them back competing at League Two level.

Above: North Terrace and Brutton's End, August 1983.

Below: Main Stand, 1990.

Address: Bootham Crescent, York YO3 7AQ

Highest attendance: 28,123 v Huddersfield Town (FA Cup), 5 March 1938

First league match: York City 2-2 v Stockport County, 31 August 1932

Final league match: York City 1-4 v Bristol Rovers, 30 April 2016

Other usages: England Schoolboys, England Youth

Ground layout: Main Stand, Popular Stand, Shipton Street End/David Longhurst Stand, Grosvenor Road End

Status: Extant

Current stadium: Bootham Crescent

Right: Popular Stand, August 1969.

Opposite top: Main Stand, August 1969.

Opposite below: Ground entrance.

York City's move to Bootham Crescent was fan-driven; their former home of just 10 years at Fulfordgate was deemed inaccessible for the City followers as it was too far from the city's railway station. The club took over the stadium from York Cricket Club in 1932. The site of York's new home was of an irregular shape and was hemmed in on four sides, with a narrow track to the south, barracks to the west, a school and almshouses to the north and terraced houses to the east.

The club had been re-formed as York City Association Football and Athletic Club Limited in May 1922 and gained admission into the Midland League. The club made its first serious attempt for election into the Football League in May 1927, but were unsuccessful as Barrow and Accrington Stanley were re-elected. However, the club was successful two years later, being elected into the Football League in June 1929 to replace Ashington in the Third Division North.

Within four months of the club's arrival, a Main Stand, running along two-thirds of the pitch, was

erected and cover was placed over the Popular Stand using sections of the terrace cover from Fulfordgate. Terraces were banked up in the wedge-shaped areas behind the goals, mainly railway sleepers hauled manually by supporters across the city from Fulfordgate. Despite the area being drained, there were problems with the pitch prior to the Second World War. During the war, the Popular Stand was converted into an air-raid shelter, and the ground suffered slight damage when a bomb landed on houses along the Shipton Street End.

In September 1948 the club purchased the ground for £4,075 after leasing it since their arrival, and supporters immediately went about concreting the Popular Stand, Shipton Street and Grosvenor Road terraces and improving the pitch drainage. Funding was supplied by the supporters' club.

The share of profit from two FA Cup semi-final ties with eventual winners Newcastle United paid for an extension to the original Main Stand towards the Shipton Street End in 1955. The following year, a concrete wall was built at the open Grosvenor Road End for over £3,000 as a safety precaution and as a support for additional banking and terracing.

Floodlights were fitted at the ground in 1959 costing £14,500, a substantial part of which was raised by the supporters' club. They were officially switched on for a friendly against Newcastle United on 28 October 1959, which Newcastle won 8–2 before a crowd of 9,414.

Seats were installed in the Popular Stand for the 1974–75 season using seats bought second hand from Manchester City's Maine Road, and the floodlights were updated and improved in 1980 for £20,000, and were officially switched on for a friendly with Grimsby Town on 1 August. Further improvements including a £50,000 gymnasium were made to the stadium in the early 1980s following yet more FA Cup success at Bootham Crescent. In January 1985 Third Division York recorded a 1–0 home victory over First Division Arsenal in the fourth round of the FA Cup, courtesy of a last-minute penalty. They proceeded to draw 1–1

at home with Liverpool in the next round, but lost heavily in the replay. The teams met in the cup again the following season, and after another 1–1 draw Liverpool again won the replay, though only after extra time.

The first issues with the ageing ground emerged around this time with cracks appearing in the wall built at the back of the Grosvenor Road End. The rear of the terracing was cordoned off, and the capacity of the ground reduced to below 13,500.

Extensive improvements were made in the summer of 1985 for approximately £100,000, and eight new turnstiles were installed at the Shipton Street End. Further, the dressing rooms were refurbished to incorporate new baths and showers, and a new referees' changing room and physiotherapist's treatment room were readied. Hospitality boxes were built into the Main Stand during 1986–87, and crush barriers were strengthened, meaning ground safety requirements were met. The Shipton Street Roof Appeal was launched in the spring of 1988 to raise money for a covered stand, and fundraising schemes were put into place.

In September 1990 York player David Longhurst collapsed and died during a match against Lincoln City at Bootham Crescent. With the approval of his family, the David Longhurst Memorial Fund was launched, and all donations were added to the monies already raised for the roof appeal. The Football Trust contributed half of the £150,000 cost of the stand, and it was constructed in the summer of 1991. The renamed David Longhurst Stand was officially opened on 14 October 1991 in a friendly match against Leeds United, which was watched by a crowd of 4,374.

The Family Stand was opened at the front of the Main Stand in 1992 and during 1993–94 the Main Stand paddock was seated down to ground level and covered, and the canopy of the roof also widened and re-angled to provide more protection against rain.

1994 saw City nearly gain a second successive promotion and enter the First Division; however,

losing in the play-off semi-finals would be their last taste of league promotion battles.

In May 1995 a new drainage system was installed for £11,000, to improve the quality of the pitch during winter, and a month later new floodlights were

installed at a cost of £122,000; despite being shorter in height they were twice as powerful as the original floodlights.

By 1999 the club had tumbled back down to the basement division. A couple of changes of dubious ownership somehow saw the ground legally separated from the club, and York were 'half an hour away from oblivion' when the Supporters Trust took them out of administration in March 2003.

The Trust proceeded with plans to move the club to the Huntington Stadium. Planning problems arose with bringing this ground up to Football League standards, and the club opted to remain at Bootham Crescent. York bought the ground in February 2004, after a £2 million loan from the Football Stadia Improvement Fund (FSIF) was secured.

The club also announced a five-year sponsorship deal with locally based confectionery giant Nestlé in which the stadium was renamed KitKat Crescent to the amusement of rival fans. The money the club received for that five-year deal, however, helped them buy back the ground.

City slipped out of the Football League in 2004, but the Trust were able to steady the ship before giving the majority stake to a businessman and fan with the financial clout to take the club further. Part of the agreement with the FSIF was for York to identify an alternative home within three years.

The club working with the City of York Council announced its commitment to building a community stadium in May 2008. This would be used by York and the city's rugby league club, the York City Knights. In July 2010 the council chose the option of building a 6,000 all-seater stadium at Monks Cross in Huntington, on the site of Huntington Stadium. In August 2014 Greenwich Leisure Ltd were named as the council's preferred bidder to deliver an 8,000 all-seater stadium, a leisure complex and a community hub.

After a nine-year absence the Minstermen returned to the Football League in 2013 but, with little work

having been done to the stadium for two decades, faced problems with holes in the Main Stand roof, crumbling in the Grosvenor Road End and drainage problems. Thankfully construction on the new stadium has started in 2016, with completion expected in early 2018. It is expected that the Bootham Crescent site will be demolished and used for housing.

Sadly, York City lost their league status again in 2016 after only three years back, and found the going very tough in the Vanarama National League. This culminated in relegation at the end of the 2016–17 season. It is to be hoped that the brand-new stadium will herald a change of fortune and that the historic city of York will host league football once again.

Below: Bootham Crescent's Popular Stand, 1975.

Opposite above: The Popular Stand in the 1970s.

Opposite below: The old Shipton Street End, 1986.

OTHER LOST GROUNDS

Brighton & Hove Albion — Withdean Stadium

The Withdean Stadium is an athletics stadium in Withdean, a suburb of Brighton. Between 1999 and 2011 it was Brighton's 'temporary' home ground, pending the building of their new stadium.

The capacity of the ground was 8,850 people, all seated.

The temporary nature of the stadium is obvious, as the stadium is primarily used for athletics; there is a single permanent stand along the north side, while the other stands are assembled from scaffolding, some of which also served as temporary seating at the British Open golf tournament. The largest was the South Stand, running the entire length of the pitch.

The east end of the pitch contained two medium-sized and one small stand. One of the larger stands here was designated as the Family Stand. The West Stand was the designated away stand. Changing and hospitality facilities were provided with portable cabins placed in various locations around the site.

Following Brighton's departure, a number of seats at the Withdean were transported to non-league's Whitehawk FC, based in East Brighton.

Bristol Rovers – Twerton Park

Twerton Park is a football stadium in the Twerton suburb of Bath; the ground opened in 1909. It is currently the home of Bath City. From 1986 to 1996 it was the 'temporary' home ground of Bristol Rovers who played there following their departure from Eastville. The stadium has a capacity of 8,840 people, with 1,066 seats.

The oldest stand is the Main Stand; this has a raised covered seating area, which means that spectators have to climb a small set of stairs to enter it. It has a steeply angled roof which points sharply downwards, with windshields to each side and a number of supporting pillars across the front. Below is a small uncovered terrace area, in front of which are the team dugouts. Beside the Main Stand is a smaller more modern structure, which is all seated, covered and has a couple of supporting pillars. This stand is known as the Family Stand.

On the other side of the ground is another weathered covered terrace that runs the full length of the pitch. At one end of the ground is a large steep open terrace that is known as the Bristol End, which is given to away fans. There is a noticeable slope to the pitch that descends from this area down to the other end of the ground. This other open end has a small shallow terrace that has nets behind in an attempt to stop balls being kicked out of the ground. The ground is completed by a set of four traditional floodlights in each corner of the stadium.

Darlington – Reynolds Arena/Darlington Arena

The Darlington Arena is a stadium in Darlington, County Durham. Since 2012 it has been home to Darlington Mowden Park Rugby Club. Between 2003 and 2012, it was the 'temporary' home ground of Darlington who played there following their departure from Feethams.

The arena was originally called the Reynolds Arena, after the club's then owner, George Reynolds.

Following Reynolds' bankruptcy and arrest on criminal charges, the name was changed to the New Stadium in April 2004. Since then the club sold the naming rights for the stadium to various sponsors. The Arena consists of four equal-sided stands. The West Stand, located behind the goal, was generally the more vocal of the two sides used by home supporters. The East Stand was allocated to away fans. The stadium is completely enclosed, with all the corners filled with seating. All the stands are single tiered and of an equal height. The stands look virtually identical apart from the South Stand, which has a row of executive boxes running across the back of it.

It was the largest Conference venue with a capacity of 25,000. Attendances for football matches were restricted to 10,000 by local planning regulations because of poor access roads around the stadium. The ground averaged a gate of around 1,500 to 2,000 supporters.

It was announced in May 2012 that Darlington would no longer play at the Darlington Arena. The club initially agreed a ground-share deal with Shildon AFC, before deciding to share with Bishop Auckland FC instead.

Newport County – Newport Stadium

Newport Stadium, also known as Spytty Park, is an association football and athletics stadium in Newport, South Wales. It is the home of Llanwern football club and Newport Harriers Athletic Club. It was also used previously between 1994 and 2012 as the 'temporary' home ground of Newport County following their departure from Somerton Park. Newport County continue to use the stadium as a base for youth teams and senior squad training.

It was upgraded to Conference standard for football and had a capacity of 5,058 prior to Newport County relocating to Rodney Parade in 2012.

The stadium is owned and managed by Newport City Council and is part of the Newport International Sports Village, which includes the Wales National Velodrome. The stadium can accommodate international-standard track and field athletic events and is of Class one standard.

The stadium has two covered stands along the touchlines of the pitch. The West Stand is all-seated with a capacity of 1,100 spectators. The East Stand is a 1,600-capacity covered standing terrace, commonly referred to as The Shed. An uncovered standing terrace also exists at the north end.

Rotherham United – Don Valley Stadium

The Don Valley Stadium was a sports stadium in Sheffield, England. Named after the river Don that flows nearby, the complex opened in 1990. It was the first completely new national sporting venue built outdoors in Great Britain since Wembley in the early 1920s. The £29 million stadium was constructed as the home stadium for the 1991 World Student Games, and it later found a variety of uses. The stadium and facilities provided a training base for the City of Sheffield Athletic Club and it was the home of the Sheffield Half Marathon.

It was also the temporary home ground of Rotherham United from 2008, following their move from Millmoor, until they moved to the New York Stadium at the start of the 2012–13 season. There were questions raised about the agreement, and the Football League stipulated that the club was obligated to move back to Rotherham within four years. Rotherham United fans were allocated the 10,000-seat Main Stand which included concourse, bar and executive facilities such as lounges and boxes. Away fans were allocated around 2,000 seats on the wing to the right of the home fans.

One of the stadium's other uses was for home games by rugby league side Sheffield Eagles; it also hosted many rock concerts given by renowned stars. At the time of its closure, Don Valley Stadium was the second largest athletics stadium in the UK and had a seated capacity of 25,000.

The track was sunk below ground level and was sheltered by banks of spectator seating, creating a 'bowl effect'. The stadium's major focal point was its grandstand which held 10,000 spectators. The main canopy roof had an area of 6,000 square metres and was made of Teflon coated glass fibre. It was supported by ladder masts reaching 39 feet (12m) above the top of the grandstand, Up to 15,000 spectators could also be accommodated on the open terracing.

There were plans in 2002 to use the stadium as a potential joint ground for the city's two football teams. In both of these eventualities the seated capacity would have been raised to 45,000. In January 2013 it was reported that Sheffield City Council were considering demolishing the stadium as part of a money-saving exercise. Despite widespread opposition, a final closure date of 30 September 2013 was set and demolition was completed in six months.

Wimbledon (2003–04) and MK Dons (2004–07) – National Hockey Stadium

The National Hockey Stadium was a sports stadium in Milton Keynes, with a nominal capacity of around 4,000 seats. This was temporarily increased to 9,000 between 2003 and 2007 for football use. On construction in 1995, it had a covered Main Stand running the full length of one side of the pitch, opposite which was an unroofed stand running about one third of the length of the pitch, straddling the halfway line.

The stadium was used first by England Hockey as their national stadium from 1995 to 2003 and then as a professional football stadium for firstly Wimbledon (2003–04), and then the re-branded Milton Keynes Dons (2004–07).

In 2003, when the ground was leased to Wimbledon, a grass pitch was laid, meaning that the stadium was out of commission for hockey. Temporary stands were added at either end of the pitch. The record attendance at the National Hockey Stadium was 8,306 for a League Cup match against Tottenham Hotspur in October 2006. In summer 2007, the MK Dons relocated to their new stadium near Bletchley (the Stadium mk) leaving the hockey stadium without a tenant. From then until late 2009, when demolition began in preparation for the site to be redeveloped, the ground remained unused. The site was cleared by March 2010. In July 2012, the new Network Rail headquarters opened on the site.

Cardiff's Ninian Park in demolition.